42 Rules for Driving Success with Books

By Mitchell Levy

E-mail: info@superstarpress.com
20660 Stevens Creek Blvd., Suite 210
Cupertino, CA 95014

First Printing: January 2009
Paperback ISBN: 978-1-60773-012-5 (1-60773-012-X)
Place of Publication: Silicon Valley, California, USA
Library of Congress Number: 2008911361

eBook ISBN: 978-1-60773-013-2 (1-60773-013-8)

Trademarks

All terms mentioned in this book that are known to be trademarks or service marks have been appropriately capitalized. Super Star Press™ cannot attest to the accuracy of this information. Use of a term in this book should not be regarded as affecting the validity of any trademark or service mark.

Warning and Disclaimer

Every effort has been made to make this book as complete and as accurate as possible, but no warranty of fitness is implied. The information provided is on an "as is" basis. The author, contributors, and publisher shall have neither liability nor responsibility to any person or entity with respect to any loss or damages arising from the information contained in the book.

If you do not wish to be bound by the above, you may return this book to the publisher for a full refund.

Praise For This Book

"There's no better way to establish instant credibility on a topic than by saying 'I wrote the book.' Mitchell Levy has established himself as Silicon Valley's author's author. Authors and aspiring authors turn to him for guidance on how to do it easily, quickly, and with credibility. In today's era of marketing turbulence, this book is incredibly relevant for anyone looking to market themselves or their brand. A must read."
Rich Goldman, VP, Corp Marketing & Strategic Alliances, Synopsys

"I always say that in order to achieve success you must first build visibility and then credibility; only then can you move forward into profitability. In '42 Rules for Driving Success with Books,' Mitchell Levy explains how becoming a published author is the ultimate way to build visibility and credibility by branding yourself as an expert which will inevitably build your business. Simply put, this book is an essential read for anyone wishing to attain a higher degree of success."
Ivan Misner, NY Times Bestselling author and Founder of BNI

"Informative and inspiring! The power of books is truly inspirational."
Karen Tucker, CEO, Churchill Club

"Nothing can accelerate your success curve faster than becoming an author. Mitchell has brought together all the secrets of 40 bestselling authors, providing the best single source for both inspiration and do-it-today advice."
Gerald Sindell, CEO thoughtleadersintl.com and Author '*The Genius Machine*' (New World Library, May 2009)

"Here's a great resource! It's a truly useful book for professionals looking to establish themselves as thought leaders. Inside you'll learn from the real-world experiences of 40 authors who describe the core components of their success with books."
James O'Toole, Daniels Distinguished Professor of Business Ethics, University of Denver, Business Week Columnist, and author of '*Leading Change*' and '*The Executive's Compass*'

Publisher

- Mitchell Levy
  http://superstarpress.com/ and http://happyabout.info/

Executive Editor

- Laura Lowell
  http://42rules.com/

Cover Designer

- Cate Calson
  http://calsongraphics.com/

Layout

- Teclarity
  http://teclarity.com/

Dedication

To my wife, Alex, who trusts that whatever I set my mind to will turn into reality and both, puts up with my long hours (which I call fun instead of work) and works alongside me in the business. To my son, Duncan, who gives me ideas and inspiration daily.

Acknowledgments

I wish to thank Laura Lowell, Executive Editor of the 42 Rules series, who is creating momentum for something big. I also wish to thank all of my support staff who make sure that things get done on a day-to-day basis. Finally, I wish to thank those who shared their stories and who live by the tenets espoused within this book.

Contents

Preface by Laura Lowell

The 42 Rules™ book series is based on the belief that most subjects can be summarized into 42 distinct areas that capture the essence of a topic. 42 Rules books can be written, and read, quickly.

For Authors, the 42 Rules structure condenses years of experience and expertise into bite-sized nuggets of information. A 42 Rules title establishes them as experts in their field and gives them a platform on which to grow a business.

For Readers, 42 Rules books quickly introduce a topic and contain tools needed to be successful.

By reinventing educational topic-based books, the 42 Rules method encourages Authors and Readers to take control, break the rules, and find strategies that work in their own lives. Since 42 Rules books are written by professionals in the field, they provide readers with insightful information that is easy to relate to and to put into practice.

I wrote my first book, '*42 Rules of Marketing*', in 2007. It was during this process that I realized that there had to be an easier way. The book had a huge impact on my consulting business—tripling revenue and increasing average project fees by almost 25%. I was amazed at how much value I got out of my book.

Mitchell Levy, CEO of the independent publishing house Happy About®, and I joined forces to provide a publication platform for the 42 Rules series, SuperStar Press. Together we help independent professionals and businesses write books that establish them as experts in the field. They use the books as platforms to grow their businesses, and create additional revenue streams and lines of business. Today, the 42 Rules series makes book publishing approachable and possible for modern day working professionals.

Laura Lowell,
Executive Editor,
42 Rules Series
http://42rules.com

Introduction

Having a book as one of your creative assets must be given serious consideration in your next marketing planning meeting.

As a marketer in today's turbulent times, you must be wondering what you can do to demonstrate your effectiveness. The key question you must be asking yourself when you wake up each morning is, "What am I going to do today to bring in more business?"

What if prospects came to you asking:

- How do I buy your product?

- Can you please speak in front of my group (e.g. your prospects)?

- Can I please get some of your brochures to share with decision makers at my company?

- I love the brochure you sent in the mail, can I please get some more?

- In a book I picked up at Amazon or Barnes & Noble, I read about your product/service. Can you tell me more?

A dream? Science fiction? No! You get all this and more with a book. You're reading this and you're excited until you think about what it takes to write a book. Then you ignore the idea because you're thinking you don't have 1,000 hours and can't wait 1–2 years to create a book. Myth!

Yes, a book published by a commercial printer will take 1,000 hours to write and 12–18 months to publish (once you secure the publisher).

But, a book published by Super Star Press or Happy About will take 60–150 hours to write and 2–4 months to publish. For a 42 Rules book (see Your Rules at the back of the book), you can have folks collaborate to help you create a book in as little as 60 hours. So the question arises, "Is a 100-page book that took 60–150 hours to create going to be effective?" The answer is a resounding "Yes!" Please read on, as many of the authors featured in this book created books that achieved amazing results. Those results are within your reach too, with a 42 Rules title to your credit!

Let me talk about the benefits of writing this book. From the time the concept was originated to the day when the book came back from content layout was 3 months. During that time, I spent 50 hours of time. Yes, just 50 hours. With the writing and other odds and ends before having a book in my hand 3 weeks from now, I would expect to have spent 60 hours. Even before publishing (see Rule 17) the benefits are amazing.

- We have 4 new authors (contracts signed) and 18 others that have expressed interest.

- We have 1 new executive editor (contract signed) who is searching for authors to write books in his series and 8 others that have expressed interest.

- We have 8 marketing firms that have put us on their radar and we've hired one of them for 2 of our authors.

Let me repeat, amazing results for 50 hours of work. Absolutely the best bizdev tool I've ever deployed!

1 Rules Are Meant to Be Broken

The 42 Rules book series is fundamentally different from other types of non-fiction business books. The writing, publishing, distribution and marketing approaches have all broken rules in order to build something unique, flexible and fast. 42 Rules books help independent professionals and business with immediate credibility and additional revenue streams. We are proud to offer Authors a unique combination of flexibility and time-to-market.

Technology has made it possible for the publishing industry to evolve. Some publishers have embraced this opportunity, and others, like the traditional "houses," have not. Traditional publishing houses still follow old processes and use expensive methods to develop, produce, distribute and market books. It takes a long time to get into the "old boys" club to locate an agent, have a manuscript be accepted, and then get published. Once you are published, it is still very much up to the Author to drive market awareness for their book.

On the other hand, online "vanity presses" have made it possible for anyone to publish a book. Typically, vanity presses have you pay for the cost of producing your book (design, production, printing, etc.) The Author is solely responsible for marketing and distribution. Typically there is no help and little support. If you have always wanted to be a publisher, and an Author, then this may be an attractive option for you.

The 42 Rules book series, and publisher Super Star Press, make it easy to write, publish, distribute and market your book. We have a 31-step book publishing process (a typical vanity press follows 10 of those steps). We can get your book to market faster, offer higher royalties and ensure that you, the Author, retain copyright to your work.

We do a number of things to help you succeed with writing, publishing and marketing your book. We focus on creating a good quality book, handling sales, logistics, and distribution. You drive content creation (except in the case of ghostwritten books) and market awareness. On the marketing side, we have created a marketing infrastructure to help you successfully marketing your book. We provide author coaching via bi-weekly Teleworkshops focused on different aspects of writing and marketing your book. We also provide extensive online marketing tools including optimized book webpages, integrated blogs, customer registration, and automated email marketing. We also have the capability to hold webcasts, create video book trailers, and develop and manage pay-per-click ad campaigns.

The truth is, Authors sell books, and we're here to help you every step of the way.

Section I
Success

Success means different things to different people. For those listed in this section, it ranges from selling 24 million copies in a series to creating 18 newsletters with nearly six million monthly readers. The titles of the rules themselves says it all:

Rule 2: Write to a Need and You Will Win (24 million copies and counting))

Rule 3: Grow Your Niche

Rule 4: Authors Don't Have to be Writers

Rule 5: Success Can Be Greater Than Imagined

Rule 6: An Investment With a Long Payback

Rule 7: Don't Wait Until You're Published to Reap the Rewards

Rule 8: Build Your Confidence

Rule 9: It Will Change Your Life

2 Write to a Need and You Will Win (24 million copies and counting)

Guerrilla Marketing has sold 24 million copies in 57 different languages. I wrote it in response to a need. If there is a need, then a book will work.

Jay Conrad Levinson, 75 ½ years old, is the father of guerrilla marketing whose books have sold over 24m copies. Visit him at http://guerrillamarketingassociation.com.

At the beginning of my career, I was a member of the U.S. Army's Counter Intelligence Corps. After the Army, I was hired at an advertising agency because I could type 80 words per minute. I rose through the ranks and became a Sr. Vice President at J. Walter Thompson in the U.S., and went to Europe to be a Creative Director and Board Member at Leo Burnett Advertising. It was the pinnacle of my career and I was earning $80K/year.

I moved to San Francisco in an attempt to make a living working fewer hours. I quickly figured it out and, since 1971, I have been working just three days a week. I recommend that to everyone. The desire to work a 3-day week and the need I saw in others to do the same caused me to write the book '*Secrets of Successful Freelancing*.' I wrote this book on a Saturday morning, self-published it, and was able to sell 300,000 copies during its life. I experimented with a ton of ideas to drive sales of the book.

I wrote another book called '*Earning Money Without a Job*,' self-published it and sold 30,000 copies before a publisher picked it up and sold a whole lot more. In 1976, I was asked to teach a course and wrote a book called '*555 Ways to*

Earn Extra Money.' An agent came to me and said that he could get me a 15K advance from a publisher for the book and I said—Go! It went well.

In the class, I was continually asked by my students to recommend a book on marketing without spending much money. I went to the library and bookstores and was surprised to find that there was nothing out there, so I wrote it myself. Originally I called it '*527 Ways to Market Without Investing Money,*' but it was just too long a title so I went with '*Guerrilla Marketing*' as it was an easier title to wrap your arms around. I never expected it to take off. To date, it's sold 24 million copies in 57 different languages. I wrote it in response to a need. I have always found that if there is a need, then a book will work—Guerrilla Marketing for Consultants, Guerrilla Marketing on the Internet, Guerrilla Marketing Startup Guide, Guerrilla Marketing for Writers, etc.

I'm currently 75 ½ and have spent the last five years in a $500K RV traveling the US with my wife. We just recently bought a place by my family in Florida. As a result of the book and the accompanying fame, I've been asked to speak in just about every nation on earth. I've spoken in Dubai, Bulgaria, Greece, Croatia, Macedonia, Serbia, Estonia, Latvia, Lithuania, Indonesia, Singapore, China and the United States.

For those who are contemplating writing, you must realize that as a writer you don't make anything. Well, it's not zero, but it's small in relation to everything else. The millions that you make will be in the doors that your book opens. My speaking fee is $55K and I manage to squeeze in some consulting at local companies around the locations at which I'm asked to speak. I'm having tons of fun—and it's all because of writing.

3 Grow Your Niche

Since the publication of the first book, ISI has grown into an Internet newsletter juggernaut with 18 newsletters and nearly six million monthly readers. It's amazing what a book can start!

JoAnn M. Laing is Group President of First Advantage's Employer Service Group and author of two books which helped drive an information company (http://hsafinder.com) serving more than seven million monthly readers.

At the turn of this century, Information Strategies, Inc. (ISI) was a growing, but little-known Internet marketing and communications company. The basis of our growth was a group of Internet newsletters whose primary audience were small business leaders. These leaders were struggling with mounting healthcare benefit costs. When Health Savings Accounts (HSAs) were introduced in 2004 as a means of addressing this problem, there was almost no fanfare and very little information available about them. Often called "medical IRAs," HSAs were little known and less understood.

Seeing an evolving marketing niche with significant potential, I sat down and wrote the first published book on HSAs. Aimed squarely at our company's primary audience—small business leaders—the book was an instant market leader, rising to the top of Barnes & Noble's listing. Titled 'The Small Business Guide To Health Savings Accounts,' the book continues to sell well despite the entry of many competitive offerings.

Building on the momentum of the book, we evolved an information-centered website and a series of seminars to educate the general public as well as business leaders on HSAs. The book provided ISI with credibility and data resources that eventually allowed it to become a "go-to" source for HSA data. ISI's reports and data are cited by government officials, the GAO, and all major media outlets.

Based on the book and the quality of its editorial on the website, government officials and industry stakeholders quickly turned to our staff to help publicize HSAs.

Working closely with administration officials, we were able to create the '*Annual White House Briefing on HSA*,' which brought together industry stakeholders and administration and congressional leaders to discuss key issues surrounding the implementation of HSA rules and regulations.

I then wrote a second book, '*The Consumer's Guide To HSAs*,' as a companion volume. Together, these two books have created a marketing channel, both online and offline, that generates advertising dollars in excess of $500,000 yearly for the healthcare sector alone as well as 4 million new readers for all of its offerings.

Since the publication of the first book, ISI has grown into an Internet newsletter juggernaut with 18 newsletters and nearly six million monthly readers. It's amazing what a book can start!

4 Authors Don't Have to be Writers

It wouldn't have happened if I didn't pay someone to push me along. What a great investment in time and money!

Robert Van Arlen is an internationally known business results speaker, author and emcee and is considered by his clients as the most engaging speaker on the planet! Visit him at http://robertvanarlen.com.

Over the past 10 years, I have spoken to numerous audiences across the country with much success. I could have never imagined how publishing a book would promote my speaking career to another level. I remember the first time I was introduced to the audience and the term "author" was included as an accomplishment in my introduction. It resonated like nothing I'd ever experienced, and I felt very proud. Though it seemed like it took forever to complete, it was a worthwhile journey.

A few years ago, I decided to slow down my pace and take the time to determine what my core message truly was. A title emerged that perfectly illustrated what I was attempting to do for individuals, teams and organizations. I wanted everyone to focus together and thus developed a concept called *Focused Synergy*, which is the title of my book. '*Focused Synergy*' provides specific guidance on vision and values alignment for individuals and organizations, both of which are critical for unifying and driving successful organizations today.

I carefully chose a writer to help me who could keep me on track and provide editorial tips to improve the flow. It was a quasi-ghost writer relationship that proved beneficial in completing the book. It wouldn't have happened if I didn't pay someone to push me along. What a great investment in time and money!

What has changed for me is the level of personal engagement that occurs during book signing sessions after I speak. Everyone has a story, and they enjoy sharing those parts of their life and career that relate to my message. Because I decided to allow my personal information to be revealed in my stories and in pictures, people relate to me more personally, and this helps us connect more deeply.

A book provides a major added revenue stream that multiplies quickly. For me, the impact has been immediate, with an increase in bookings of more than 50 percent over last year. Not bad for a supposedly down economy! Orders come in daily from various sources, and at least twice a month I get an order for 100 or even 1000 books. Many clients choose to buy books prior to events, so they have them on hand when I speak. Fortunately, as a self-published author, I have greater flexibility to include a predetermined number of books as part of the package, and I sometimes do. Ultimately, a book is the greatest marketing tool you can develop and the ROI is limited only by your imagination.

I've also seen my credibility grow exponentially as an author. The word "author" seems to conjure the professional connotation of being an expert. Companies love to hire experts, and being published provides enormous confidence in the fact that you believe in your own message when you take the time to publish your concepts. Also, leaving books with my audience helps build momentum for additional referrals and more book sales.

While writing and producing a book can be long and tedious work, the benefits you gain from it, such as increased revenue stream, improved credibility and the elevation to expert status can grow your business exponentially. I found it not only personally satisfying, but also professionally profitable.

5 Success Can Be Greater Than Imagined

This book has helped YogaFit became the largest yoga education program in the country and made me an internationally renowned exercise expert who has trained more than 100,000 fitness instructors on six continents.

Beth Shaw is President and Founder of YogaFit and author of the book 'Beth Shaw's YogaFit.' Visit her at http://yogafit.com.

I have been fired from every job I've had before I founded YogaFit in 1994. After practicing yoga since 1989 and taking several Yoga Certifications, I began teaching at fitness clubs in Los Angeles. I soon discovered that, while traditional certifications taught a lot about the history and philosophy of yoga, they did not address the nuts and bolts issues of teaching yoga in a health club. Knowing the many challenges of teaching yoga in a health club—bright lights, cold rooms, bodies of all types and fitness/flexibility levels, I created my own style of yoga that combined fitness moves such as push ups, sit ups and squats with traditional yoga postures linked together in a flowing fitness format. To make the practice user-friendly I eliminated the Sanskrit names of the postures and avoided the 'OM'ing and chanting sometimes associated with traditional yoga practices. YogaFit was born.

YogaFit's Teacher Training program began in 1997, but after I wrote my first book titled '*Beth Shaw's YogaFit*' in 2001, the company took off. The book was a great alternative for people who could not make it to classes or trainings. For others, it made them want to get up and try YogaFit for themselves.

YogaFit and the training program have expanded over the years, and now feature internationally renowned programs for training fitness professionals in YogaFit. YogaFit has Teacher Trainings Level One, Two, Three, Four and Five, in addition to over 40 specialties. YogaFit has a 200 and 500 hour Registered Yoga Teacher (RYT) program. Before Level One trainees can receive their Certificate of Completion they are required to perform 8 hours of practice teaching in a community service setting. Trainees have brought the practice and benefits of yoga to seniors in long term care homes, stressed-out corporate executives, cancer patients and survivors, disabled persons, incarcerated persons, terminally ill persons, children, mentally challenged individuals and military servants, just to name a few.

Thanks to the success of the book, YogaFit became the largest yoga education program in the country and I am now an internationally renowned exercise expert who has trained more than 100,000 fitness instructors on six continents. *'Beth Shaw's YogaFit'* brought speaking opportunities at conventions, thousands of loyal trainees and customers and has served as an educational tool for those who cannot make it to YogaFit conferences and weekend courses.

I also publish *Angles* magazine, which is distributed to yoga fitness enthusiasts and instructors. Myself and YogaFit have been showcased in numerous fitness magazines as well as in *Time, More, Entrepreneur, Yoga Journal*, and *USA Today*. I've also been featured on CNBC, CNN, NBC, CBS, E Style Channel, Showtime, and *Donny Deutsch's Big Idea*. All this from one book...success beyond my expectations.

6 An Investment With a Long Payback

The ROI from the items where I could put a value itself was easily north of 10X.

Rajesh Setty is a serial entrepreneur, investor and author based in Silicon Valley. Visit him at http://blog.lifebeyondcode.com.

My first book was published when I was thirteen. It was a murder mystery. Before I turned sixteen I had published three more novels, a collection of poems and a book on mathematics for college students. None of these were books that would demonstrate any thought leadership on my part. I was young, and at that point in time it didn't matter much. It seemed like getting a book published at that age was sufficient to create buzz and leverage.

Thirteen years later, I started a company in Silicon Valley. It was not my first company by any means. I had one failed and aborted attempt at a startup back in India. I didn't want to fail again. For those of you who remember the year 2000, it was a tough period for any startup to survive, as nobody was buying anything from anyone and everyone was trying to sell anything to anyone.

There were exceptions, but it so happened that we were not in that category. The more I observed how things worked, it became clear to me that "who you are" in the marketplace and "who you are connected to" are equally important as compared to the offers that you are making. A powerful personal brand would have provided the boost that I badly required.

That was one of the motivators for me to write my book *'Beyond Code: Learn to Distinguish Yourself In 9 Simple Steps'* (foreword by Tom Peters). This would be my first step to establish my thought leadership and personal brand.

During the same time I started my blog called 'Life Beyond Code' mostly to support the book. Of course, the blog has now become bigger than the book with more than 1,100 articles on Entrepreneurship, Leadership and Living a Life Beyond Code. The book has done reasonably well in the United States. A year later, the Indian Edition was published by a well-known Indian publisher, and is doing well there too.

While I made only a few thousand dollars in royalties from the book, the indirect benefits from this and related exercises have been huge. Being a business professional, I calculated the ROI by putting assigning numbers to the indirect benefits (examples: new opportunities, speaking engagements, new relationships) over the last few years. There is no way I can assign a value to many things that showed up for me. For example, I was able to build new relationships with wonderful people over the years and they will be friends for a lifetime. I can't assign numbers to those relationships; they are invaluable. The ROI from the items where I could put a value itself was north of 10X, easily.

Bottom Line—I have thought about this investment of time, energy and money on writing a book to build a personal brand and establish thought leadership. The verdict for me is clear—I wouldn't have it any other way.

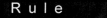

7 Don't Wait Until You're Published to Reap the Rewards

Besides saving a large client (who is worth between $20,000–$40,00 0 per year in income), the pre-release endorsements for the book have resulted in appearances on major news networks...

Vicki Kunkel is author of 'Instant Appeal: The 8 Primal Factors that Create Blockbuster Success' and runs the firm Be a Power Player (http://beapowerplayer.com).

Like so many subject matter experts, my first book, soon to be published, 'Instant Appeal, the 8 Factors that Create Blockbuster Success' (AMACOM, November 26, 2008), came about when one of my clients said, "You should write a book on your research!"

I put it off for over two years. Writing a book? Who has time when there are clients to see, pitches to make, requests for proposals to respond to, speaking engagements to go to?

All I wanted the book to do was to be a well-researched, interesting, cutting-edge source of information on the concept of "stickiness" and mass appeal. What I got was far more.

As I write this, it's mid-September, 2008. My book won't even be released until late November. But already that book increased my annual income by $46,000.

One of my major long-term clients, who had been with me for years, called me in June with some bleak news. "Vicki," he told me, "I love your work. We all do here. You've made a huge impact and we've seen measurable, positive results from your work. But the powers that be say we need to look for a communications expert with a lower fee. The economy's bad and budgets are tight..."

I gave him my best pitch, but he said his hands were tied. So, I thanked him for the many years his company had been a client, and thought this would be the perfect time to ask for a favor.

"Say, John, since you know my work, could I send you the draft manuscript of my new book and, if you like it, would you provide an endorsement? I already have endorsements from people like Brian Tracy, Jay Conrad Levinson, Marshall Goldsmith, and some other major players in the professional development market." He agreed.

Three weeks later, I got a call from this same guy who said, "I loved your book. So did my boss. The research is outstanding. I'll send the endorsement to you along with a contract for you to train 23 of our field representatives on Instant Appeal selling techniques." I thought I had misunderstood. "Beg your pardon?" I stammered.

"I passed your manuscript along to my boss, and he now says that we can't afford not to go with you," he replied. "I can't cut my rates to match the lower-priced vendor," I warned. "You don't have to. Your expertise warrants your rate."

Besides keeping a large client (who is worth between $20,000–$40,000 per year in income), the pre-release endorsements for the book have resulted in appearances on major news networks, as well as a job offer from a news organization wanting to know if I would be interested in doing freelance science reporting, which I am seriously considering.

You never know what a book will do for your career.

8 Build Your Confidence

Smooth Sale is now an LLC, my products are branded, my confidence is at an all time high—and I just submitted a second manuscript to my publisher...Without my book, I would no longer be in business....

Elinor Stutz is a corporate sales trainer, motivational speaker and author of the book 'Nice Girls DO Get The Sale: Relationship Building That Gets Results.' Visit her at http://smoothsale.net.

In 1992, after being a stay-at-home mom for 15 years, I entered a blue collar sales office to sell an unknown brand of copiers door-to-door. The men did everything imaginable to force me out. There was no training, I knew nothing about business or the technology, and I was so green that I did not even know there was a sales cycle. All I knew was I would not be forced to quit.

Everywhere I landed an appointment, I asked personal questions, personal goals and then business goals. By the fourth month, I became the top producer and held that title through my career on into high-tech. Business became so unethical at the end that I quit to begin my own company, Smooth Sale.

Once again the men wanted me to prove myself and women ran away from me when I said "sales trainer." I began to read marketing materials day and night and they all said, "Write a book!" So I wrote a corporate tell-all.

At first, I self-published it. The moment the book was printed a male business associate challenged me by saying in a nasty voice, "If your book was any good, a publisher would have picked it up!" I did not want one last doubting male ever again.

I hired an agent to find a publisher. Sourcebooks picked up the book and titled it, '*Nice Girls DO Get The Sale: Relationship Building That Gets Results.*'

Readers write to say the stories are laugh-out-loud funny (it wasn't funny at the time) and they read the book with a highlighter in hand because it contains so much valuable information.

My book was featured in TIME Magazine, translated into multiple languages and sells worldwide. It landed me countless business opportunities including training in numerous corporations, coaching hundreds of folks over the phone, speaking at many large conventions, and creating a full product line to complement my books. I've also been interviewed on ABC-TV KGO "San Francisco View On The Bay" and on 24 other radio shows. My book launched the Sweet Success Book Club and I've had the opportunity to contribute articles to Diversity Edge Magazine and Women's Connection magazine.

Smooth Sale is now an LLC, my products are branded, my confidence is at an all time high—and I just submitted a second manuscript to Sourcebooks!

Finally, there is no doubt in my mind that the single best thing anyone can do for their business is to write a book and get it published. Without my book, I would no longer be in business—it had that dramatic an effect by providing the credibility I so badly needed.

9 It Will Change Your Life

Yes, it offers credibility, but it allows new prospects to really get to know me and what I can do to help them change their lives and businesses.

Jen Blackert is a business and life coach and author of the book 'Seven Dragons: A Guide to a Limitless Mind.' Visit her at *http://jenblackert.com.*

Many people have asked how I became a writer and how authoring my books has changed my life and my business. My name is Jen Blackert and I am a business and life coach. I have authored two books and I am a contributing writer to many others over the past three years. To say it has some effect on my business would be a complete understatement. The truth is that my business has grown from being a so-so business to a profit-growing machine that just keeps getting better every single day.

My first book, 'Seven Dragons: A Guide to a Limitless Mind,' was written out of a need to save time. I had been working with business clients day in and day out and had found myself continuing to share the same stories and concepts. One day, one of my clients jokingly said that I should write a book. I pondered it for a moment. It was a great idea. Hmmm...instead of being a broken record why don't I write these stories and experiences for my clients to read—what a concept!

I didn't realize at the time what I had started. I found that clients would read the book and then purchase a bundle of books for their staff and then those people would further share it with their friends and family.

After the small viral success, I decided to try an Internet book campaign. I sold nearly 1,000 books in a week and six months later the book is still selling strong. My business success is completely due to the success of this book. Yes, it offers credibility, but it allows new prospects to really get to know me, and what I can do to help them change their life and business. I have found it to be a great way to introduce myself to new prospective clients instead of trying to sell myself to them.

After looking at the success of '*Seven Dragons*,' I thought I would see what would happen with a second book that includes more of a practical side of business. So, I wrote a marketing book. It's a book that includes both mindset and marketing. It demonstrates how I use simple strategies to market my business.

I had no idea how it would go over, since I was marketing it to a list of prospects that purchased my first book on mindset. Well, I had so many pre-orders that my publisher had to issue a backorder request. It seemed like many of the people who purchased my first book purchased my marketing book and the other books I have contributed to.

The funny thing is that the books are very simple and straightforward. They are only simple, honest stories and basic concepts. Due to their success, I am going to continue to write. I hadn't ever really thought of myself as a writer, but it is starting to sink in now. So what's next for me? I am off to write my next book on wealth creation and then I am going to write a sappy, girly novel.

If you even have an inkling of a thought to write a book. I would say... don't think about it anymore... just do it!

Section II
Growth

A book (or book series) will grow your business. The stories in this section focus on:

Rule 10: Books Belong in the Marketing Mix

Rule 11: Have the World Come to You!

Rule 12: Referrals Find You

Rule 13: Each Book Opened Another Door

Rule 14: This Book Transformed My Business

Rule 15: Create a Powerful Calling Card

Rule 16: Market Me Automatically

Rule 17: It Closes Business

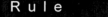
10 Books Belong in the Marketing Mix

I began writing books ten years ago. I never envisioned the difference it would make in my fees as well as my "stature" as a speaker.

Marsha Petrie Sue is a professional speaker and author of four books, including 'Toxic People.' Visit her at http://MarshaPetrieSue.com, http://DecontaminateToxicPeople.com.

As a professional speaker, I am always looking for ways to increase my bottom line without having to increase the amount of time I spend on the platform. In addition, I have found that many people want to extend my message to their work groups and teams. So I began writing books ten years ago. I never expected the difference it would make in my fees as well as my "stature" as a speaker.

My first three books were self-published. The last one, *'Toxic People: Decontaminate Difficult People at Work Without Using Weapons or Duct Tape,'* was published by John Wiley (New York). I continue to be amazed how this book has put me on a very different level from other speakers. The book is a Barnes & Noble bestseller and also a #1 on the CEO Read list. Publishers from Russia, Romania, and France have requested the rights to publish the book in their languages. The distribution has been worldwide.

My fees have increased, and my bookings are way up, not to mention the money being made from the sales of the book. My speaking fees went from $3,500 to $5,000 for a keynote presentation when I self-published *'The CEO of YOU: Leading Yourself to Success.'* We are now publishing the 4th edition of this book and have sold over 35,000 copies. When 'Toxic People' was released, my fees went to $7,500 and then quickly moved to $10,000 for a keynote.

To continue this momentum, I hired a Public Relations firm, Robert Smith (3pr@ureach.com), to help with the promotion of the book. Because of his expertise, I have been interviewed and written up in The Wall Street Journal, Investors Business Digest, The New York Times, Cosmopolitan, The Christian Science Monitor and many more.

We continue to promote the book, write press releases and maintain visibility in front of business people who have to deal with difficult people constantly. What I have learned is that when you have a media request, you must immediately follow up with the person inquiring.

When I was asked to speak to the US Army, I asked the chairperson for the event how they found me and she said that her boss had read my book, 'Toxic People!' She said that the book became a hit in the office and was purchased by everyone. Interestingly, my sessions at their event were standing room only and the majority of the people attending said they were there because they had "heard about the book and how helpful it was!"

Another very useful application for the book is using it as a business card. When a Speakers Bureau or Meeting Planner requests my speaker packet, my book, along with my demo DVD is FedEx'd to them. We do not send the packets by regular mail. I have been told by recipients of the packages that it distinguishes me from others. Also, when I receive the delivery confirmation email from FedEx it gives us one more reason to contact the client and follow up.

11 Have the World Come to You!

The first thing the caller said was, "I remember your CAREER book..."

Joyce Schwarz is a futurist, new company launch consultant and Hollywood strategist. Visit her at http://joycecom.com, http://hollywood2020.net, http://ihaveavision.org.

Let me start off by saying that being the author of a published book changes your life for the better. It does so by creating a new reality where the world comes to you if you plan it right. '*Successful Recareering*' catapulted me into the national eye—a 10-city book tour, PBS TV, NBC news interviews, two articles in the Wall Street Journal, and a two-page spread in the L.A. Times.

The bottom line was over $250K in free promotion/advertising for the new firm I was launching as well as my existing marketing business. The Center for Successful Recareering company still exists today and turns an annual profit solely based on word of mouth marketing.

I parlayed my prominence in multimedia into a $500K grant for retraining from the State of California for one of my clients: a Cal State college. Not only was this lucrative for my company, but it aided in providing training for thousands of engineers and others into the new media industry, so it was personally rewarding too!

The first week my '*Multimedia: Gateway to the Next Millenium*' trade book was published by Harcourt Brace, I picked up the launch of Hasbro online as a consultant.

Asked later by a major telecom company to present a proposal for consulting on their new wireless division, I sent my 'Cutting the Cord' book which led to my being hired for a six-month consulting gig.

At the moment, my newest book from Harper Collins Publishing, Collins Design, is the #1 Spiritual Bestseller on Amazon.com (http://ihaveavision.org). And not only did I wrangle a six-figure advance with similar bonus structure my agent and I created, I'm also using the book as a launching point for a) a venture funded company b) a Hollywood inspirational film and video development c) the launch of a direct selling organization for personal development materials (not unlike an AVON for self-help).

Just recently, a top-tier Executive MBA program called me to be the keynote speaker for this 'Fall's orientation—eaturing hundreds of top execs from Fortune 100 firms who are going back for their MBAs. Why did I get the call? The first thing the caller said was, "I remember your CAREER book." Can I parlay it to preview my new book and an info-media line of products? Sure. So, I received a fee for speaking which was nice; more importantly I got an opportunity to speak in front of hundreds of incoming MBA's...priceless.

With my success with books, it is no wonder that I've encouraged and coached 38 of my clients to publish books. I've motivated another 25 to produce theatrical films and hundreds to create CDs and DVDs for their vertical of expertise.

12 | Referrals Find You

Since completing my book, referrals find me. My closing ratio and hourly rates are higher...

Jim Muehlhausen CPA, JD, is President of CEO Focus (http://ceofocus.com) and author of 'The 51 Fatal Business Errors' and 'How to Avoid Them.'

Unlike many authors, I never intended to write a book. The bulk of my career has been as a business owner and for the past nine years as the head of CEO Focus, a peer consulting organization for local business owners. As the head of CEO Focus, my responsibilities include: marketing peer group membership to CEOs in my local market, coaching and consulting with those CEOs, and traveling the country helping CEO Focus franchisees successfully launch in their markets.

In support of these activities, I created many workbooks, pamphlets, and white papers to reward CEOs for their attendance at our workshops. Over time, I compiled these into a 51 Fatal Business Errors Workbook. The response to this workbook, which I was cranking out on my Epson printer, was fine. It was meeting my needs by demonstrating my organization's intellectual property. However, it lacked the pretty packaging and sizzle of a full-fledged book.

Then I met a local author whose entire consulting business was centered around his book. One hundred percent of his prospects were generated from his book. The prospects who read his book were much easier to close as consulting projects. When I saw the book, I said,

"Wow, my 51 Fatal Errors Workbook is meatier than this!" I set about turning my hodgepodge collection of materials into a "real" book. Over the next six months, I turned the materials into what is now a successful business book, '*The 51 Fatal Business Errors and How to Avoid Them.*'

Quite frankly, the authoring process was nothing like I expected. Everything I thought would be easy was tough. Everything I thought would be tough was easy. Would I do it again? Absolutely, and I have already begun my second book. Why would I do all that work again when the profits from the book sales will only pay for a couple of nice dinners per month? It's simple. The credibility gap between, "I am a smart guy with some materials" and "I am a smart guy with a book" is astronomical. Simply stated, a book is the best business card you can have.

Since I completed my book, referrals find me. My closing ratio and hourly rates are higher. The bottom line: you probably won't make any money selling your book but the marketing leverage you will create for yourself and your business is beyond quantification. Since I have "seen the light," I have nearly a dozen clients in the book writing process. Their specialties might surprise you: a collection agency, software development, ad specialties, business coaching, staffing, importing, etc. I strongly encourage you to make the investment in a lifetime asset and the ultimate business card.

13 | Each Book Opened Another Door

I repackaged my ideas into a one-day course, set an appointment with Shell's decision maker, and won the contract 100% because I was an upcoming author of a book that fit their need.

Dianna Booher, MA, CSP, CPAE is a prolific author with over 44 books; her firm works with organizations to increase their productivity and effectiveness through better oral, written, interpersonal, and cross-functional communication. Visit her at http://booher.com.

I started writing a few articles and, as luck would have it, the first article submitted was accepted. Being new to the business, I thought, "this is how it works, I send something, they publish it." I soon received my share of rejections, too, but I was hooked. Soon an editor saw an article of mine and asked me to turn it into a book, which Simon & Schuster/Messner then later turned into a series of books for young adults.

Several years later, I taught a novel-writing course at a local community college. I surveyed students and asked them why they were taking the course. To my surprise, many were from companies in the surrounding area and were actually hoping to improve their business writing skills, and novel writing was the closest thing they could find.

I jumped at the chance to fill this obvious need and began writing my first business book, '*Would You Put That in Writing?*' Meanwhile, I solicited additional input from others on how to appeal to business clients. One friend, a Vice President at Shell Oil, mentioned that Shell was paying "big bucks" to have a vendor teach writing to their engineers and lawyers. Driven by the opportunity to meet a business need, I repackaged my ideas into a one-day course, set an appointment with Shell's decision maker, and won the contract 100% because I was an upcoming author of a book that fit their need. This bold move helped launch my company, Booher Consultants, Inc.

Not long after Shell hired me, my writing book hit the shelves, followed closely thereafter by a grammar book. (The newest version is '*E-Writing: 21st Century Tools for Effective Communication*,' available at http://booherdirect.com). The *Houston Chronicle* ran a feature story about it, and on that day when I called the answering service to check for messages (yes, this was before voicemail and email) the operator said, "Ms. Booher, I don't know what you did, but you've had 32 calls this morning." All those callers were interested in my book and what I could teach their employees about business writing. I was soon leading courses and delivering keynotes to companies around the globe.

With the success of my writing workshops, it wasn't long before a client, ConocoPhillips, asked me about teaching a presentation skills class. The new curriculum was a natural move as my extensive teaching and speaking events offered the perfect means for fine-tuning my presentation techniques. And, not surprisingly, the request paved the way for a new book, '*Speak with Confidence*.'

IBM needed to improve customer service communication across the organization. So, guess what? Booher's eService workshop and corresponding book, '*Communicate with Confidence*,' were born. Technical writing? Ditto. Email communication? Ditto. Again and again, I listened to the needs of my customers and allowed demand to drive the response.

These days, in addition to running my company, I typically write two books a year. Because other authors often ask how I get it all done, once or twice a year I share my secrets in a 3-day publishing workshop. No matter what motivates people to write—money, marketing a new service or product, promoting their professional expertise, passion for a topic—there are things they have to learn in order to get their books into print. In my Get Your Book Published workshop (http://GetYourBookPublished2009.com), new authors learn everything from writing a proposal to marketing their book for creating spin-off products, to using their books to promote their businesses. I love to share my passion with new and experienced authors. "We all start somewhere, and the best never stop learning and growing!"

14

This Book Transformed My Business

Over the years I've found that there's nothing like handing a prospective client a book with my name on the cover to establish instant credibility.

BJ Gallagher is a Los Angeles-based consultant, author, and speaker. Visit her at http://peacockproductions.com.

Steps to Success was the name of my business. I was in the corporate training and consulting business, having been the former training manager for a large metropolitan newspaper. I liked the alliteration of Steps to Success, and I also liked the practical, how-to implication. People can *learn* how to achieve success and I wanted to teach them the steps.

But within six months of starting my business, I realized that I was still carrying a lot of resentment and anger toward my former employer. I thought that writing about it would be cathartic—allowing me to purge those negative feelings, get rid of the old baggage, and move on with my new business.

I started to write. My story was titled '*A Peacock in the Land of Penguins*' because that's how I felt while working in my corporate job. I was a colorful, entrepreneurial, noisy bird working in a stuffy, bureaucratic, good ole boy organization. The Very Important Penguins (VIPs) liked my productivity and accomplishments, but they didn't like my peacock style. It was a very frustrating, painful work experience.

Writing my story seemed like a good mental health exercise. Little did I know then how it would change my life!

After many rejections from all the big New York publishing houses (populated by penguins, I might add), my peacock story landed in the hands of the publisher/editor of a small San Francisco publishing house, Berrett-Koehler. They were committed to transforming the world of work through the business books they published, and my oddball bird book was a perfect fit for them.

In 1995, '*A Peacock in the Land of Penguins: A Fable About Diversity and Discovery*' hit the bookstore shelves. It wasn't a runaway success, but its momentum built slowly. Each year, the book has sold more than it did the previous year.

My co-author, Warren Schmidt, and I decided to adapt the book into an animated training video for corporations to use in their diversity seminars. We partnered with a talented animator and got busy. When the video was complete, we decided that support materials would be helpful to trainers, so we designed assessment tools, training manuals, and workshops for others to use in their organizations. One thing led to another and soon we had a veritable cottage industry built around the book and video. Penguin coffee mugs, penguin stress toys, T-shirts, book bags, feather pens, and more—I was surrounded with a plethora of penguins and peacocks!

Fast forward to today...the third edition of our Peacock book is now published in 21 languages worldwide, with sales over 300,000. It is THE best-selling diversity book in the world! It wasn't too long after the book was published that I realized the birds were taking over my business, so I changed the name to Peacock Productions. Today, virtually ALL of my business revolves around penguins and pea-cocks—my speaking and training business, as well as sales of videos, books, and training materials featured on my website.

Over the years I've found that there's nothing like handing a prospective client a book with my name on the cover to establish instant cred-ibility. So I tell all my consultant and trainer friends that they should consider writing books. It's a great career enhancer and business builder. And if my friends say that I'm for the birds, I smile and reply, "Yes, and I've got a nest full of golden eggs to prove it."

15 Create a Powerful Calling Card

While it's unlikely that anyone who purchases my book will read it cover to cover, it absolutely sets me apart from other single-shingle management consultants who have just a business card.

John Honeycutt is a Principal and Founder of xBig6.com and author of the book 'Provocative Business Change.' Visit him at http://xbig6.com.

In 2005, I self-published *'Provocative Business Change'* which I wrote while I was an independent management consultant. The book has subsequently been a powerful calling card for me. There are three key roles my book has played.

- First, it helped me land a leadership role at a major consultancy

- Second, in helping to gain increased credibility with a previous business contact resulting in a $1.2 million signed statement

- Third, as a marketing asset for an independent consultant launching a new consulting business; xBig6.com

While it's unlikely that the reader will read my book cover to cover, it absolutely sets me apart from other single-shingle management consultants who have just a business card. I'm able to ship a copy directly from Amazon, which most people are somewhat impressed with (even today).

The book itself is a good "personal reference builder" and "credibility maker." Additionally, the act of putting my thoughts on paper crystallized my point of view and forced me to think through the "what, how and why" of my consulting. I'm able to use these points in my discussions, and having a copy of the book to open a page to and refer to in my PowerPoint presentation makes discussions much more consequential.

In addition to the points above, I've used the book in the following ways:

- I've spoken seven times for utility industry leaders from October 2006 through July 2008. The credential of "author" was useful in the first few speaking events, to get on the agenda.

- While working on an ERP implementation, twelve copies of my book were provided to an existing client undergoing significant acquisitions and growth. Partially due to the book, which elevated my expertise in transition planning and change management, I was tagged to lead a new piece of business with the client for $500K.

- The book has served as a relationship builder and excuse to remain in contact with a few dozen business contacts especially those I had not done a good job of keeping in contact with otherwise. In two distinct cases, I've been able to rekindle decade-old relationships into support and business.

While it's just a little ritual, people I talk to want me to sign my book. They know I'm not some important author, but I think it's more like getting a great holiday card or gift. In signing their book, I'm able to write something kind which gives me one more opportunity to have a quality interaction with a client or potential client.

16

Market Me Automatically

Michael Soon Lee is a multicultural expert and author. Visit him at http://EthnoConnect.com or call 800-417-7325.

In one case I got a call from a new planner who said, "I just found your book in my office as I was moving in. This is exactly the information that our members need."

In 1985, I wanted to be a great motivational speaker like Tony Robbins. I had been an entrepreneur and university professor, so I figured the transition would be easy. Unfortunately, I got lots of rejections. However, as I would turn to walk away, meeting planners would always ask, "Do you speak on diversity?" To which I replied, "No, I'm a fifth generation Chinese American whose family has been in the United States since 1855. What would I know about diversity?"

Eventually, I changed my tune and started speaking about how to sell homes to minority customers. Multicultural sales became my specialty and, in 1999, I wrote a book just for real estate agents entitled '*Opening Doors: Selling to Multicultural Real Estate Clients*.' Its popularity led to hundreds of speaking engagements at local, state and National Realtor Associations as well as real estate companies.

It's amazing how much more effectively my book marketed me, as compared to a business card. In one case, I got a call from a new planner who said, "I just found your book in my office as I was moving in. This is exactly the information that our members need." Another person call with an apology, "I'm so sorry. My boss gave me your book to review to see if we should carry it in our bookstore. I got so engrossed in reading how culture can affect the way people buy that I highlighted and made notes all over and I can't return it like this. Could you send me another book? By the way, I hire all of the speakers here and would love to have you present to our group." These and countless other opportunities would never have happened if I'd just sent a letter.

As a result, I qualified to become the first Asian American in the history of the National Speakers Association to earn the Certified Speaking Professional designation, and my book raised my fees. One planner who balked at my fee said, "We usually don't pay speakers this much but because you're an author..."

Then, someone asked me to write a book just for new home salespeople, so I adapted my content for that market and this best-selling book has led to many presentations in the building industry. Next, a credit union asked me to write a similar book about how to market to multicultural credit union members.

Over the years people have asked me to speak to new car dealerships, insurance companies and even hospitals about how to attract multicultural customers and provide them with stellar customer service. In 2008 Wiley Publishing asked me to write a more generic book for salespeople in all industries called 'Cross-Cultural Selling for Dummies.'

I have also taken concepts from my first book and expanded them into other books. For instance, I wrote 'Black Belt Negotiating' published by AMACOM Books. This gave me the credibility to go back to many of my original clients and speak about negotiating.

As you can see, I owe my success as a professional speaker to my first book. I only wish I had written it sooner!

17 It Closes Business

If I only knew what a significant impact it would have on my business, I would have done it years before. Using the book as my business card, we closed an astonishing 93% of the work we bid. It was just amazing.

Thomas G. Martin is President of Martin Investigative Services and author of the book 'If You Only Knew.' Visit him at http://martinpi.com.

A few years back, a publishing company came to me and asked me to write a book about some of my most famous cases as a former supervisory federal agent (DEA) and as a private investigator. I said no at first because I was not sure that anyone would care nor did I see how that would help me monetarily or in generating business. Reluctant at first, *'If You Only Knew'* was given "birth" about six months later in the form of a self-help book with each chapter having a significant story byline. If I only knew what a significant impact it would have on my business, I would have done it years before.

During the past decade, my colleagues have been competing in an unfair playing field. Although there are over one hundred thousand (that is right, 100,000) private investigators in the U.S., only a small number are making a significant income. Using the book as my business card, we closed an astonishing 93% of the work we bid on. It was just amazing. We all dressed, spoke and presented ourselves well. Some would leave cards and a brochure. I would leave a copy of my book with the favorable review we received from the Los Angeles Times. I would sign each book to the person or persons within the company doing the interviewing. Deal closed.

In the international arena, the percentage was closer to 100%. They didn't need to read the book, as many cultures were sufficiently impressed with the discipline to start and finish a book. Having traveled to over 120 foreign countries, I was astonished to learn their feelings. Many times the interview would stop and a retainer check was provided.

We then did a book tour, appearing in over 70 television shows and 700 radio shows. Sales of the book were great but pale in comparison to the investigative work we generated with corporate America, attorneys, insurance companies and the public.

We are now known as "America's PI," in great part to the book. This year we updated the book. One of our computer people at the corporate office suggested I put the book online for free. We did that last month and it has proven to be a marketing "sensation" all over again.

Section III
Credibility

Thought leadership means different things to different people, but one thing is clear. Being an author of a book gives you the title 'Thought Leader.' Read how these authors used that title to drive success for them and their businesses.

Rule 18: Be The Thought Leader

Rule 19: Get a Ph.D.

Rule 20: The Press Sees You Differently

Rule 21: From Nobody to Somebody…BIG

Rule 22: Become the Instant Expert

Rule 23: Stand Out as an Expert in a Crowded Field

Rule 24: Become a Recognized Speaker in Your Field

Rule 25: Get Immediate Credibility

Rule 26: Redirect Your Energies & Efforts

Rule 27: Cement Your Expert Status

Rule

18 Be The Thought Leader

My first book took me out of the role of "trainer" and into the role of "thought leader."

Marshall Goldsmith is one of the world's foremost authorities in helping leaders achieve positive, measurable change in behavior and has been ranked by the Wall Street Journal as one of the "Top 10" consultants in the field of executive development. Visit him at http://marshallgoldsmith.com.

One of my earliest mentors was Dr. Paul Hersey, the author who developed the term "situation leadership." He said something that took me 12 years to internalize and act upon. He said, "You're very good at what you do, but you're too good. You're making too much money. You're running around selling your days and successfully selling too many of them."

Even with those words in my head, I spent the next 12 years selling my days. I never built my brand and I never went to the next level with my career. Essentially, I had enough money satisfying my existing customers.

Once I started investing in the future, the payoff was immediate. My first book was '*The Leader of the Future*' which I published through the Drucker Institute. This book took me out of the role of "trainer" and into the role of "thought leader." Just one book and I started building my long-term brand.

At that stage, I set the goal of being the world's leading authority in achieving successful change and books were a significant component of hitting that goal. I realized that I needed three things:

- I needed to deliver a message (always had that)

- I needed content (came from writing)

- I needed credibility (came from writing)

The message and the ability to be listened to was always something I was always good at. Books gave me the missing two pieces and have made a significant change to my life.

My best-selling book is 'What Got you Here, Won't Get you There' which has sold over 250,000 copies. Once you write a global bestseller, people know who you are. You get more calls, more opportunities and, more important, you are asked to work with high-powered people with more interesting stories.

I'm one of the few people in the field who measures success. I get paid when my clients get better. Period. So, there is a direct correlation between my efforts, my clients' performance, and my pay.

I can say that there is a direct correlation between who I am today, the work I do, and the money I make, and being an author. I've had a gradual uptick for the last 12 years from my first book. My fees are 4–5 times what they used to be. My current speaking fee is $35K/day. Books have been very, very good to me. If you want to be an important person in my field, you must write one.

19 Get a Ph.D.

I'm not sure my own business would even exist as a viable enterprise without my various books.

Shel Horowitz specializes in affordable, ethical, and effective marketing for authors and publishers, small businesses, and nonprofits. His latest books are 'Grassroots Marketing for Authors and Publishers' and 'Principled Profit: Marketing That Puts People First.' Visit him at http://frugalmarketing.com or call 413-586-2388.

Until you experience it, it's hard to imagine the kind of career boost you can get when you have at least one book with your name on the cover. I'm not sure my own business would even exist as a viable enterprise without my various books. Not that the books are a primary revenue stream for me—but they open so many doors that would be much harder to get through without those credentials, and they more than pay their own way through actual orders.

Books are the easiest way to certify your expertise. If you have a book out, you're assumed to know what you're talking about. You're the expert—the one who wrote the book on the topic. This makes it not only easier to convince prospects to become clients, but also gets you noticed by reporters and meeting planners who hire speakers.

A book is the easiest doorway to media coverage, with all its benefits. Thanks to my books, readers of publications as diverse as the *Christian Science Monitor, Entrepreneur,* the *Los Angeles Times, Reader's Digest, Bottom Line,* and *Woman's Day* (among dozens of others) all know about me. And thanks to my books, I've also been featured on the home pages of msn.com, aol.com, and paypal.com, among others.

Books give you something to display and sell at your website, your speaking engagements, trade fairs, and a gazillion other outlets. Something eye-catching, if you've got a good cover.

When you have a book, you pretty much have automatic access to (and exposure on) high-traffic websites such as Amazon.com and Google.com—access that would cost you big dollars if you had to pay for it.

The actual cost of a book to you is very low compared to its perceived value. This makes it an ideal gift to business associates whom you'd like to impress, as well as something to give away and get visibility when you attend Chamber or other business meetings. I usually donate a book and then, when the executive director draws the business card of the lucky attendee, I stand and wave, and then make contact with the winner and offer to sign and personalize the book—and perhaps this is one reason why I've gotten several clients out of my local Chamber. I've also raffled off books when I've attended national conferences where nobody knew my identity until the book was given away.

A book gives you an entry point to start relationships with movers and shakers in your industry: consultants, reviewers, e-zine or newsletter publishers, conference organizers, and successful entrepreneurs. People who hire assistants to screen their email and correspondence will often be happy to receive a book as a gift, and may even lend an endorsement or order copies for friends; it sure beats hanging out at the front gate of their mansion until security comes to haul you away.

Books, if they're useful, informative, and well written, encourage people to send work to you. I can't tell you how many times I've answered the phone to hear something like, "I've been reading your book. Do you ever do any private consulting (or speaking)?"

Finally, a book provides several possibilities for adding directly to your bottom line. Of course, you can sell books directly to your clients or customers. But you can also sell them to meeting planners who can give or sell them to attendees...get a nice fat check if a foreign publisher decides to publish your book...sell bulk quantities (sometimes thousands at a time) to corporations and associations...the possibilities are endless.

The Press Sees You Differently

Expert status was not conferred on me by experience, at least not experience alone. It was conferred on me because I wrote a book.

Mark Amtower is the founding partner at Amtower & Company. Visit him at http://FederalDirect.com, http://GovernmentMarketingBestPractices.com.

I started Amtower & Company in 1985, specializing in compiling targeted lists of key senior people in several job categories in the Federal Government. Snail mail was a major marketing tool at the time, and when I added consulting and speaking to my list of services, it seemed like my toolkit was complete.

By the mid-1990s, I was a recognized leader in marketing to the government, but something was missing. When I spoke at a Direct Marketing to Business (DMB) conference in 1994, it became clear *what* that was. During Q&A after my presentation, an attendee asked when my book was coming out, as my presentation had more useful information in one hour than most business books. I explained I didn't have one...yet.

The seed was planted, but it took another 11 years to come to fruition. That was a major error on my part. In January, 2005, once '*Government Marketing Best Practices*' was published, the media separated me from everyone else. Although I was quoted more than anyone else before the book came out, I was usually referred to as "a government marketing consultant" or "partner at Amtower & Company." When the book came out, phrases like "government marketing guru Mark Amtower" started showing up in places like BtoB magazine. Expert status was not conferred on me by experience, at least not experience alone. It was conferred on me because I wrote a book.

It helps that there are not many "doing business with the government" books on the market. It also helped that my book, like the session delivered at DMB in 1994, was full of practical information, not theoretical platitudes. It sold well for a self-published book.

Two years after the book was out I got a call from a friend who was at a conference. He was in the back of the ballroom where a Small Business Director from a major federal agency was speaking. My friend called to tell me that this small business person was addressing the audience, holding my book up and saying, "I don't know this guy, but if you want to do business with my agency, you need to read this book." In this market this is the kind of endorsement you cannot buy. Unfortunately, it is also the kind you cannot use, which is why his name and agency are omitted here.

As a result of that call, I contacted this small business office and indicated that if the director was serious, I would sell the agency books well below the cover price, as long as they bought in bulk. I tiered my case pricing accordingly: 1–5 cases at 50% off the cover price (I would still be making over $9 per book), 6–9 cases at 55% off, and over 10 cases at 60% off. They called back to ask if I could lower the price a little for 20 cases—just over 1,000 copies.

Since then, this agency is responsible for ordering over 4,000 copies. I have also sold in bulk to corporations that sell to the government. Suffice it to say 'Government Marketing Best Practices' is not a NY Times bestseller, but it is by far the best selling book in the government market.

The great thing is the book was not designed to be a profit center—it was designed to position me as *the* expert in marketing to the government. With the tacit endorsements from major corporations and government agencies, this mission is accomplished. The real profit comes from the consulting driven by the book (send a copy of *your* book to a CEO, and they'll take your next call!), and having a monthly fee membership website with the book title.

From Nobody to Somebody...BIG

Rather than being one in a thousand, I'm now sought out (by people what have seen the reviews, heard the podcasts, etc.) as a recognized authority. And guess who gets the job...

Mike Brookes is the author of 'The Real Secrets of the Top 20%—How To Double Your Income Selling Over the Phone.' Visit him at http://MrInsideSales.com.

There are a lot of sales trainers out there, and even more motivational speakers. Trying to differentiate myself and my company by defining my niche (Inside Sales), offering great content and information with a weekly e-zine, and creating an outstanding website all had an impact and helped me attract some business, but most days it was a struggle to get noticed. That all changed when I was approached to write a book sharing my expertise and techniques.

Having never published a book before, I was skeptical and had a lot of questions. Would I have enough information to write a book? Could I even write? How would I be able to afford the marketing? What kind of marketing would I do? What if nobody even bought the book? How would it help me and my business? These were just some of the questions I had in the beginning, and I found that I had many more as I got into the process.

The good news, and the biggest piece of advice I can offer someone thinking of publishing a book, is that if you find the right publisher (someone you can talk to and work with; someone with experience who knows the process well; someone who has your combined interest in mind; and someone who is passionate about your book) then everything will fall into place and in no time you will have a finished and valuable product that can catapult you and your business. Here are some of the immediate benefits a published book has provided me:

1. **Great networking.** While putting my book together, my publisher urged me to reach out to other professionals in my business to get testimonials. At first, I didn't think competitors would want to help me, but this turned out to be a great way to network and to develop relationships that have already helped me run my business more effectively.

2. **Amazing exposure!** Since my book has come out, I have been contacted to do interviews, podcasts, articles, and it has opened up other marketing opportunities I never would have had access to otherwise.

3. **Increased business.** Having a published book has suddenly made me an authority in my niche market (and in sales in general). Rather than being one in a thousand, I'm now sought out (by people what have seen the reviews, heard the podcasts, etc.) as a recognized authority. And guess who gets the job when I'm bidding on something someone who quotes books, or someone who wrote the book?

4. **Incoming calls.** Just while I was writing this (all true, I'm NOT making this up!), I had a call from someone who just bought and read my book. He is opening a company and needs help with scripting, training, etc., and last week I received a call from a business owner who ordered two copies of my book a month ago, and they have now hired me to do an in-house all day training event.

Bottom line? Having a published book has completely changed my business because it has driven business to me. And once those inquiries come, I no longer have to convince or sell myself; my book does it for me. If you're thinking of writing a book to help your company get noticed and get more business, then start today. Believe me, it's the best thing I've ever done to promote and grow my business, and it will be for yours, too.

22 Become the Instant Expert

I was on TV around the country as the expert on small businesses...al l the free PR created through interviews on radio and TV and in the press saved us hundreds of thousands of dollars in advertising expenses....

Marc Joseph is President of Dollardays.com (http://dollardays.com) and author of the book 'The Secrets of Retailing.'

Dollardays.com was started to help small business survive and thrive against the big chains. The next channel of distribution for wholesale and closeout products to reach small businesses was going to be the Internet. This last vessel of true guerilla marketing provided a level playing field where small businesses could get the information and products they needed at the same time major chains were procuring the goods. Our marketing on the Internet was productive, but how could I get the word out to the masses of entrepreneurs and business owners who had yet to experience the efficiencies created by buying online? This was why my book was born.

Small businesses are virtually ignored in the big business world we live in. Manufacturers and wholesalers can't afford to spend time on an order under $1,000. The urge to be an entrepreneur in this country continues to be strong, but the support system that existed when small business was king is dying.

Because I realized that support to small businesses was hard to come by and using the Internet to help build your business was just emerging as a sustainable business, my book *'The Secrets of Retailing: How To Beat Wal-Mart'* was published in 2005 by Silverback Books to fill the void in information on how to not only build a business from scratch, but how to integrate the newest technology with your brick and mortar business to sell successfully beyond your local trading area.

I launched the book with signings in several bookstores, including independent bookstores as well as Borders. I was interviewed on 221 radio shows across the country in both major markets and smaller markets giving us a chance to reach out to our customer base of small business owners without having to pay for advertising. So, bottom line, all the free PR created through interviews on radio and TV and in the press saved us hundreds of thousands of dollars in advertising expenses. I spoke at several conventions around the country and continue to be asked to speak today.

The book helped to get the message out that this was absolutely the best time in America's history to be an entrepreneur and start your business. It also helped to start my brand, http://dollardays.com. It helped catapult us into the Inc. 500 list of the 500 fastest growing privately owned businesses in 2006, where we landed at #158.

Bottom line, the book brought awareness to a part of our economy that does not make the headlines everyday. Entrepreneurship is strong and thriving in this country and I am proud to be a part of it.

23 | Stand Out as an Expert in a Crowded Field

I started to get calls and emails from reporters...they all wanted to talk to me. Why? Because I was the guy who wrote the book on LinkedIn.

Jason Alba is CEO of Jibber Jobber and author of the books, 'I'm on LinkedIn—Now What???' and 'I'm on Facebook—Now What???' Visit him at http://JibberJobber.com/blog.

I started a bootstrapped company in September of 2006. With no formal marketing training or experience, and with very little capital, I did what I could figure out to market my website. I became an avid blogger, and implemented an aggressive blog-marketing strategy, which proved to be very beneficial on a number of fronts.

I thought I had kind of hit the top of my blog marketing strategy, and was looking for ways to create more buzz, get more attention, and attract more eyeballs and users. Over a dinner meeting I asked a couple of authors some questions about their books, and the process of writing and publishing their books. I was interested to know what kind of revenue they generated from book sales, and wasn't really interested in speaking or consulting. I shared a book idea with one of the authors, who then introduced me to his publisher, Happy About.

From that meeting, I became convinced that I should write my book, which might generate some income and would definitely fill a need that my JibberJobber users had. But I had no idea what the real benefits of being a published author would bring.

Once my book came out, I started to get calls and emails from reporters who were interested in interviewing me about LinkedIn. I wondered why they didn't call the experts who had been consulting on LinkedIn for a while, but they all wanted to talk to me. Why? Because I was the guy who wrote the book on LinkedIn.

I quickly learned to say how I wanted to be attributed, which was always Jason Alba, CEO of JibberJobber.com and author of *'I'm on LinkedIn—Now What???'* Because of these interviews, I saw my name, and my company website, mentioned in places I had always dreamed of getting mentioned in. The credibility I got from being mentioned in those magazines and newspapers was something I had been seeking since I started JibberJobber, but it took my book to actually make it a reality.

A few months later I decided to write a second book, *'I'm on Face-book—Now What???'* One of the major benefits I got out of that book was that I was no longer "the LinkedIn guy," or "the job search guy", rather I was become known as an expert in social networking and social media. This has expanded my brand, led to more interviews and exposure, and branding for JibberJobber.

I used to say that blogging was the most significant thing I have ever done for my business, with regard to marketing. That used to be true...up until I became a published author.

24 Become a Recognized Speaker in Your Field

By 2007, I found my passion in front of an audience and I realized there was a real story to tell.

Lisa DiTullio is the principal of Lisa DiTullio & Associates, a training and consulting practice dedicated to introducing project management as a business competency, enabling organizations to improve decision-making, accountability, and communications. Visit her at http://lisaditullio.com.

I didn't find my calling in life until I reached middle age. Up to this point, I was quite fortunate. I had a fulfilling career. My strong work ethic and desire to succeed helped me advance to upper management status and I was paid well. But at age 45, I knew I wanted more. Call it what you will; I knew I needed to do more before the opportunity went away. I yearned to be in front of an audience.

As past director of the project management office at Boston-based Harvard Pilgrim Health Care, I was the core member of the turnaround team for an organization that went from being placed in State-supervised receivership in 1999 to being named the #1 Health Plan in America on the U.S. News & World Report/NCQA America's Best Health Plans three years in a row.

While at Harvard Pilgrim Health Care, I pursued professional development opportunities by seeking public speaking engagements. In 2005, I began submitting speaker proposals to many conference producers, all within the project management industry. Over the next few years, I became an active member of the speaking circuit, sharing battle scars and triumphs through my experience in a turnaround situation.

By 2007, I found my passion in front of an audience and I realized there was a real story to tell. Audiences were both awed by the turnaround story and educated on the information I provided through best practices and lessons learned. The real writing began in January of 2007; the story was ready to be told. It took a mere three months to complete the first draft. My decision to self-publish was based on many factors, including the ability to publish quickly.

My book, '*Simple Solutions: How Enterprise Project Management Supported Harvard Pilgrim Health Care from Near Collapse to #1*' hit the shelves on November 15, 2007—just in time for my appearance at a large project management conference held in Orlando, Florida. The book sold out during the pre-conference seminar; attendees were placing orders for the remainder of the weeklong conference.

In February 2008, I left Harvard Pilgrim Health Care to establish my own practice, Lisa DiTullio & Associates. Being a published author gave me the credibility I needed to leave the comfort of a large corporation behind. Today, in spite of a challenged economy, my practice is thriving. My speaking career has attained new heights by increasing four-fold over the last year. I have finally reached a level where people ask me to speak at their events, rather than me always seeking the next opportunity. I can now call myself an international speaker—I have traveled to five countries in the past year alone. All of these engagements have fueled my practice. In spite of a challenging economy, I am confident in my ability to succeed.

My 2nd book is underway—this is just the beginning.

25 Get Immediate Credibility

When you have written a book, people think you know something they don't. That's not fair....

Sharon Armstrong is the founder of Sharon Armstrong and Associates and author of three books—'The Essential HR Handbook,' 'Stress-free Performance Appraisals,' and 'Healing the Canine Within.' Visit her at http://TheEssentialHRHandbook.com.

I hadn't planned on writing 'Stress-Free Performance Appraisals' back in 2002. But when an agent at Career Press read my first book—a humorous account about my dog Scooter and his dog friend Max called 'Healing the Canine Within: A Dog's Self-Help Companion'—she liked it, and thought I could write another book for her.

This one was for HR professionals, and right up my alley, for I had been in the business since 1985 when I worked as a recruiter/trainer in a large Manhattan law firm. I then took over as Director of HR at the DC firm Shaw, Pittman, Potts & Trowbridge in 1991, and in 1994 became the Director of HR and Administration at the Association of Trial Lawyers of America. In 2000, I opened my own firm, Sharon Armstrong & Associates, and since have trained scores of professionals and completed HR projects for hundreds of clients.

Writing for the industry that I knew and loved was a relief because selling the first book had been an interesting experience. Although my co-author and I spent many a night eating take-out Chinese, drinking wine, and laughing our way through the manuscript, we were a little disappointed when 11 of the 12 publishers our agent sent it to turned us down—except for Ballantine Books at Random House, which published it in 1998.

Nonetheless, I was smitten by the idea of publishing books, so I gave writing the second one a try. I collaborated again—this time with strategic communications professional Madelyn Appelbaum—and we also had a ball writing it.

Fortunately, my experience this second go-round was incredible—mostly because it provided me something that I hadn't expected: immediate credibility.

Once the 224-page paperback hit bookstores, it took off like gangbusters. I soon received countless calls from organizations that wanted to become clients, and my income took a jump to 6-figures for the first time.

What amazed me, too, was that dozens of human resources professionals from across the country booked me to come in and speak about the art of stress-free performance appraisals.

Here's the hard truth: when you have written a book, people think you know something they don't. That's not fair, because plenty of human resources professionals who work inside companies certainly know how to do performance appraisals. The reality is that someone from the outside a company always gets a little more respect than those closer to the belly of the beast.

Add to that a signed copy of a book, and you magically have instant credibility.

26 Redirect Your Energies & Efforts

To make a book work, it takes an ego, a realization that it needs to become your new business card and the courage to redefine and redirect your efforts and energies in the short run to expand your business organically for sustainable growth in the long run.

Joshua Estrin is CEO of Concepts In Success, a consumer marketing and branding firm and author of the book 'Shut Up! And Listen To Yourself.' Visit him at http://conceptsinsuccess.com.

As a successful Entrepreneur and CEO/Founder, I was used to breaking all the rules while growing my business development firm, Concepts In Success, which grew out of an amalgamation of a network of remarkable contacts made during my years securing a dual Master's from Columbia University, as well as a knack (I am told), for simply spinning straw into gold.

But something was missing...the equation was working but, as I learned in 8th Grade Chemistry, it was not a balanced one...What did I need? A BOOK.

Dubbed a "Charismatic Leader" by traditional leadership models, I embraced the "gift of gab" but wondered if it would transfer to the printed page. While I have known many who have benefited greatly from utilizing the expertise of a ghostwriter, I decided the demographics I had identified, the successful yet "worried well" would appreciate and benefit from my conversational tone and "anti self-help" approach to taking one's personal and professional life to the next level in the only voice I knew, mine.

Initially the formula was simple—get it published and get out there using it as a springboard to become the "go to guru" for all things business related. "Back of House" sales were the focus, using online portals like Amazon and Barnes & Noble to support the brand.

With the book published, I was a young Social Entrepreneur with a laser focused approach to P&L and ROI who was now taking on the likes of Dr. Phil and doing it between the covers of my book, '*Shut Up! And Listen To Yourself*' with radio and television on my heels.

What was my secret? It may "take a village" to raise our children, but to make a book "work" it takes an ego, a realization that it needs to become your new business card and the courage to redefine and redirect your efforts and energies in the short run to expand your business organically for sustainable growth in the long run.

My business development firm was suddenly catapulted into the limelight and a new market vertical. The creation, synergy, traction and reaction of the book by the business community and media (e.g. It was in the swags of the 2004 Oscar's after party) engendered a new niche for us—that of Public Relations. Suddenly, I was the "go to guy" to get your product and services "on the radar" and my "story" was proof that anyone could do it.

Five years later and with appearances on all the major networks, a host of two radio shows and hundreds of mentions and "madness" in print, I have been lucky enough to still have the distinct honor of being coined the founder of the "Anti-Self Help Movement."

I have used and "abused" my book to support several charities, as it has become my calling card and a new calling; *my book* has allowed me to share my model of change in a way that transcends the simple tenets of business rhetoric and instead allows me to stand out in the crowd, book in hand.

One part entrepreneur, a dash of ego mania, and heapin' portion of "I double dog dare you" has allowed for unprecedented growth of my company and taken me not only "outside the box", but most important-ly, *beyond the box.*

Live it, breathe it and most importantly NEVER apologize for having written it.

Cement Your Expert Status

The handbook, which cost $70,000 for both editions, earned my business a payback of more than $250,000 and counting.

Guy Maddalone is the nation's household help expert, and president and founder of GTM Payroll Services Inc. Visit him at http://gtm.com.

Every day, I see positive results from publishing my handbook *'How to Hire a Nanny: A Household HR® Handbook.'* First published in 2003 and a second edition printed in 2006, my handbook is a comprehensive guide for people finding, hiring and retaining a nanny and other household help, such as elder care provider, housekeeper, gardener, etc. In short, the handbook helps people be a successful household employer. It offers easy-to-access guidelines, examples, practices, procedures, laws and regulations. Your home is your most important organization, and effective household management contributes to the smooth and sound operation of your home.

Increasing awareness of the household employment industry was the book's primary goal—which it accomplished significantly. Before this handbook, there was a dearth of information regarding how to do household employment right. Considering the number of high profile careers extinguished because people mishandled their household employment, i.e., nannygate, the handbook was and is much needed. My timing is on target, as more and more Americans' attitude toward household employment is changing—and it will continue to change as more and more people consider hiring household help as a way to balance their personal and professional lives.

The handbook was helped by a tremendous wave of press coverage when the book first launched—and it continues today. The media attention, which includes media bigwigs *Wall Street Journal, the New York Times* and *Inc. Magazine,* cemented my position as the nation's household help expert. Now, the press contacts me as the go to source for such topics.

The handbook, which cost $70,000 for both editions, earned my business a payback of more than $250,000 and counting. Available through Barnes & Noble, Borders, my company website and several other book retailers, the handbook:

- Spurred customers to purchase more products, which resulted in a higher ticket price for the book

- Helped us launch a new help desk service

- Led to a new product for our clients—preparation of their own employee handbook through a self-propelled software program (like Turbo Tax)

- Generated 100+ new business leads in its first year alone

- Created speaking opportunities and meetings with a number of Fortune 500 companies, which led to multiple clients

- Is being released via a leading publisher of self-help legal books, moving our business into another market

Prominent business leaders Jack Welch and Bill Gates have copies of the book. I started out writing a book to dispel the myriad misconceptions regarding household employment and all this has come from it. It's been a great project.

Section IV
Branding

Whether you're a large corporation or an individual service provider, a book could provide you with the branding you need to be successful.

Rule 28: Immortalize Your Ideas in Books

Rule 29: Turn Your Story Into a Book; And Your Book Into a Business

Rule 30: Be a Pioneer

Rule 31: Find Your Passion and Make It Your Life

Rule 32: Create a New Business From Writing a Book

Rule 33: The Power of Your Autograph

Rule 34: Brand Yourself

Rule 35: Expand Your Marketing Platform

28 Immortalize Your Ideas in Books

> I told myself, "If I live for only a few months, I want to make sure my ideas live after me...."

Judith E. Glaser is pioneering change agent in the consulting industry that has introduced her powerful transformative technologies to CEO's and their teams at major Fortune 500 companies. Visit her at http://benchmarkcommunicationsinc.com.

Writing '*Creating WE: Change I-Thinking to WE-Thinking and Build a Healthy Thriving Organization*' and '*The DNA of Leadership*' changed my business and career dramatically, moving my work and ideas around the globe.

I'd thought about writing a '*Creating WE*' book since I was 14 years old. At the time, the title I selected was '*No Man is an I-Land.*' Fortunately, the title was taken and in any case, I only had 1½ pages of wisdom to share.

Twelve years ago my dream returned. I put together a 30-page document of my best thinking about how "WE-centric" workplaces triggers Vital Instincts—basic human instincts for co-creation. I worked on this book idea for three years with the help of a developmental agent. Publishers began to warm on the idea but ultimately rejected all 20-book proposals we sent out. They felt my idea of using neuroscience as a business metaphor would not sell and couldn't see where to place the book: Medical section? Business Section?

Rejection after rejection took its toll on me. I put my dream on the shelf one more time.

On Sept. 11th, 2001, at the same time the World Trade Center was under attack, I was being diagnosed with Breast Cancer. When you give up on a life's dream your cells know you have given up the fight to bring your voice into the world, and my body suffered. Cancer was my wake-up call and brought me back to life. I told myself, "If I live for only a few months, I want to make sure my ideas live after me."

Chemo took away my hair and my courage. I forced myself to attend a women's luncheon, wearing my wig. Hugging the walls, my eyes locked on a woman I needed to meet. Julie Huss, a writer with two books under her belt, became my muse. By asking me provocative questions about my ideas, she helped me turn my initial 30 pages into a 250-page book.

Then I met my next angel. Book collaborator Judy Katz gave my first draft a new patina. She also introduced me to my agent, who found me my publisher Al Zuckerman, who fell in love with the concept of "WE-centric Leadership" so much that they even created a new imprint around my books. *Creating We* sold well, and has already been translated into Chinese, Spanish, and Korean.

My second book, '*The DNA of Leadership*' came out 11 months later, and also found its way around the globe to an incredible practitioner named Louise van Rhyn. *DNA and me* were invited to South Africa where we did keynotes at the University of Stellenbosch and in other business venues.

Creating We became a new buzzword among my clients and in the press. DNA offered a new paradigm to business people to help them language the illusive, yet most important side of business: how environment shapes our brand, leadership and culture. My life changed overnight. My books were in demand. My ideas were attracting attention. My appearances on NBC, FOX TV, and hundreds of other radio, TV and print media brought back a tsunami of interest in my work. Adams Media, who took the risk, had helped change my life.

In 2007, I launched the *Creating We Institute* to take this work out into the world. We have universities, including Harvard, Kellogg, Univ. of Chicago, Temple and more, coming to us for new insights, which are fundamentally based on integrating neuroscience research and psychology into business.

Books have been very, very good to me!

Turn Your Story Into a Book; And Your Book Into a Business

I turned my message into my book, and just having that 117-page hardback book led to more speaking engagements.

Steven Wiley is an entrepreneur, acclaimed international speaker and founder of The Lincoln Leadership Institute at Gettysburg and author of the book 'The Human Side of High Performance.' Visit him at http://lincolnleadershipinstitute.com.

I have had the great honor of being invited to speak at some of the biggest organizations and Fortune 500 companies in the world to make presentations based on a book I wrote during the toughest period in my life. It is called *'The Human Side of High Performance*,' and I am thrilled to say that its message has resonated with some of the most famous, and infamous, leaders of our time, who have hired me to speak to their sales teams and managers.

I didn't just wake up one morning and decide I wanted to be a celebrated author and speaker who helps people be more productive and effective as sales and business professionals. I began by trying to help myself.

Back in 1989, the company that I started after graduating from Gettysburg College in 1973 with a $600 loan—the one that made millions and landed me on the covers of *Entrepreneur, Inc.* magazine, and *USA Today's* Money section—lost $4.7 million. In 1990, it lost even more. In that historic year in my life I had 16 major litigations going on in 11 states and two other countries. I also had 387 smaller accounts go to collection.

My teeth gave out, too, and in those two years I had four root canals, was 50 pounds overweight and was taking two kinds of blood pressure medicine. I knew I needed to make some significant changes if I was going to survive.

By 1991 my company started making money again—but I was on a new mission. My friends encouraged me to share my lessons learned with other business leaders, and their support helped me land speaking engagements at some of the world's largest corporations. I turned my message into my book, and just having that 117-page hardback book led to more and better speaking engagements.

Thousands of managers, educators, sales directors, and C-level executives have passed through our three-day training workshop called "A Transformational Journey from Gettysburg" based on the book. We use the lessons learned from the bloody Battle of Gettysburg, where 50,000 men died in three days and some unlikely leaders ultimately helped the North prevail.

While planning the curriculum for the Journey series, I found a quote from President Woodrow Wilson, and to this day his words are my mantra: "You are not here merely to make a living. You are here to enable the world to live more amply, with greater vision, and with a finer spirit of hope and achievement. You are here to enrich the world. You impoverish yourself if you forget this errand."

At this stage, our business is exploding to the point where we can't even keep up. This is a good thing. I plan on penning three more books, which will bring us to a completely new level—it will be fun to watch.

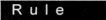
30 Be a Pioneer

These books along with much media attention drove awareness to the industry and my agency. Actually, they were two of the best marketing tools I've ever implemented.

Michelle Dunn has over 20 years experience in credit and debt collection. She is the founder and president of her Credit & Collections Association, Never Dunn Publishing, LLC, and is a writer, publisher, and consultant. Visit her at http://michelledunn.com.

I worked as an accounts receivable clerk for many years before being promoted to credit manager. Once I had cleared up the bad debt at that job, I moved to a company where I was able to write and implement a credit policy for the entire corporation. That work provided the foundation for the book '*Become the Squeaky Wheel.*' I left the company to start my own home-based collection agency (M.A.D. Collection Agency) in January 1998 and ran it successfully until I sold it in December 2004.

Another entity I started and still run today is a ten-year-old online association for credit and business professionals (Credit-and-Collections.com) with thousands of members. With this Association, I have generated thousands of loyal members who recommend the association and my books. Additionally, it has significantly helped the industry grow and learn.

While running my agency, I published two books whose content helped people create their own collections agencies and provided great marketing tools for my business. Actually, they were two of the best marketing tools I've ever implemented.

These books along with much media attention, drove awareness to the industry and my agency. More and more people started thinking about starting their own collection agency. There were no books on the subject at the time, which absolutely helped their success. As "the" author on the topic and a pioneer on the field, I was the expert, which positioned me as a leader. This attention created leads that turned into paying clients. I obtained over 100 new inquiries about my services and approximately 75% of those turned into paying clients. Many of our new customers wanted to use an agency that had an expert and leader at its helm.

As I wrote more books and the agency continued to do well, the demand for me to speak at business functions increased. Success was so staggering that I decided to sell my collection agency and write full time.

I have showed hundreds of people how to start and run their own credit and collection business. I have some of their success stories on my website. After selling my agency, it freed me up to start a publishing company and I continue to write and publish books to help entrepreneurs and business people worldwide. My books, networking group, and websites have contributed significantly to my success.

As a result of these books, I have been repeatedly featured in *The Wall Street Journal*, *Smart Money Magazine*, Forbes.com, *Ladies Home Journal*, *Home Business Magazine*, *Entrepreneur*, Professional Collector, Credit & Collections Risk, the NH Business Review and in many business books. I have been a featured guest on National Public Radio (NPR) and have been in many newspapers and magazines nationwide as well as on the CBS Early Show, Process for Profit and The Book Authority.

31

Find Your Passion and Make It Your Life

Officially an author, I landed speaking opportunities, got invited to share my insights through interactive workshops and created an entirely new career.

Bonnie Ross-Parker is the CEO/Founder of The Joy of Connecting® and author of 'Walk In My Books: The Joy of Connecting.' Visit her at http://BonnieRossParker.com, http://TheJOYofConnecting.com.

After years of networking and through the encouragement of others, I came to the decision to write a book about my experiences in the desire to help others in their own business networking challenges. I, too, had attended business after hours, endless Chamber events, and women's organizations involving casual networking, with full lunch or dinner followed by a speaker. Lame at best and with everyone shoving a business card in your hand, I didn't find any of these events particularly rewarding, effective or productive. No one was really listening to what I had to say or my 'elevator' speech because they were too busy doing all the talking. This scenario is played out everywhere.

The counterpart to this form of networking is the leads group. The same individuals get together every week to reiterate the same pitch to the same audience and then pass leads. Leads are counted to determine how many new leads were generated. Some may call this effective and for those who do I say, "terrific." As for me, I found both the business networking and leads groups to be flat, predictable and ineffective. Instead of focusing on what I didn't like, I decided to write a book about what I knew would be more productive, build stronger relationships and generate bottom line results. *'Walk In My Boots: The Joy of Connecting'* resulted.

In 2003, I established my own publishing company and got to work. My book focuses on connecting. I invite the reader to journey with me as I share insights, ideas and stories of how connecting with ourselves, with others and with the world creates lasting value. Increased results occur when we support and honor each other and when we feel connected to those whose lives touch our own. Readers learn how to attract people and build profitable relationships, increase their network of contacts, learn to stand out in a crowd and much more. With new perspective, networkers are armed with a new approach.

'Walk In My Boots' was the catalyst to unexpected activity. Officially an author, I landed speaking opportunities, got invited to share my insights through interactive workshops and created an entirely new career for myself. I earned the accreditation to become a full member of the National Speaker's Association. Emails and letters poured in as readers uncovered new ways of networking by implementing my ideas to strengthen their resolve. While written from a woman's perspective, I was flattered to hear from men who shared that they were communicating more effectively with female clients because of my approach! That was an unexpected development!

My efforts didn't stop with the book. After years of mentoring, I decided to expand beyond my relationship with my readers and create a venue specifically for women to network with one another in a unique format. The Joy of Connecting® became a licensed program for women who are serious about growing their businesses. Women meet in a licensee's home, socialize over dinner and then each participant gets to share her story, distribute materials and connect with the others at a much deeper level than at typical events. Leaving with a complete roster in hand, attendees have expanded their warm market, attracted potential new customers and feel better about themselves for having experienced a productive evening.

32 Create a New Business From Writing a Book

The exposure from publishing these books has led to further professional and personal rewards. Our initial project has grown into our own business and website.

Paula Jablon and Ellen Vacco are workplace educational consultants who have written two books. Visit them at http://eslworksolutions.com.

We didn't set out to write a book. We were educational consultants and taught English as a Second Language for twenty-five years. As the demand for workplace programs increased, we were asked to design curricula and develop programs for a number of different work sites. Frustrated by the lack of substantive material and in order to meet the needs of our students, we created exercises, stories and dialogues related to their specific jobs and the American workplace in general. After many years our colleagues finally persuaded us that others in the field would benefit from our knowledge and expertise. So we decided to write our first book, '*At Work in the U.S.*'

From the beginning, writing the book was a collaborative effort which was personally rewarding for both of us. We were equally committed to the project and our different personalities and writing styles enhanced the task at hand. Furthermore, the knowledge each of us had gained from working with different students, supervisors and management provided us with a broad understanding of the workplace and limitless ideas and material for our book.

The professional rewards from writing have been numerous. Publishing '*At Work in the U.S.*' gave us the recognition we needed to advance in our careers. Soon after its release, we were asked to give a presentation about the book and workplace education to the national organization for ESL teachers (TESOL). We had additional requests for similar presentations at Chambers of Commerce, various work sites and educational programs, as well as regional and state organizations; and the demand for our work tripled. Also, as a result of the success of 'At Work in the U.S.,' we were asked to write another book, 'Conversations for Work.' To date, thousands of copies of our books have been sold worldwide.

There are some other less direct but significant rewards as well. Workplaces with ESL programs using our materials have reported significant gains in worker morale, teamwork and adherence to rules and policies as well as successful completion of training or retraining programs. Our programs have received several achievement awards, and work has increased by 30%. Also, as a result of these successes, we have further expanded our programs to include workshops for management. They are designed to help supervisors and managers accommodate and better understand the needs of their immigrant workers, with a long-term goal of greater productivity.

Finally, publishing these books has led to establishing our own business and website, http://eslworksolutions.com. As our business grows, we hope that our books will continue to help workers develop the language and cultural awareness they need to be successful.

The Power of Your Autograph

I love signing books and giving them to patients because it gives me a chance to write a comment that will inspire them and help them to feel better about themselves and their lives.

Jay P. Granat, Ph.D., is a psychotherapist and founder of StayInTheZone.com and author of multiple books. Visit him at http://StayInTheZone.com.

In 2008, World Audience, Inc. released two books I wrote: '*How To Get Into The Zone In Just One Minute*' and '*Zone Tennis*' that builds on the success of my previous works: '*How To Get Into The Zone With Sport Psychology And Self- Hypnosis*,' '*How To Lower Your Golf Score With Sport Psychology And Self-Hypnosis*,' '*Bedtime Stories For Young Athletes*,' and '*101 Ways To Break A Hitting Slump With Sport Psychology*.'

My books have generated hundreds of thousands of dollars in sales around the world. They have been purchased by people who want to learn how to perform to their fullest potential. Customers use these books and programs to help stay calm, focused, self-confident and optimistic. The books teach people how to get into the zone and stay there.

I have coached baseball players, basketball players, golf pros, professional bowlers, boxers, martial artists, hockey players, skaters, tennis players, fencers, wrestlers, gymnasts, swimmers, divers and track and field athletes. I've also counseled rodeo cowboys, poker players, professional fisherman, CEO's, and traders who want to develop their peak performance skills.

The books and related programs have helped me land interviews on Good Morning America, The Canadian Broadcasting Company, The British Broadcasting Company, ESPN radio and many other media outlets. I've also been quoted in The New York Times, The Newark Star Ledger, The Bergen Record, Executive Golfer Magazine, Associated Press and other major print media. Golf Digest named me one of America's top ten mental gurus. I also write a weekly column for three newspapers and am featured in a documentary film about the psychology of long distance running, called 'Beyond The Epic Run.'

This awareness building the books has helped create allow me to counsel elite athletes, parents of top athletes and coaches around the world. Writing the books has given me a chance to collect my thoughts and to disseminate useful information to my target audiences, to my colleagues, and the public in general. I enjoy writing and plan to write two more books in the next twelve months.

Writing has definitely helped to build my platform and enhance my image. I also love signing books and giving them to patients because it gives me a chance to write a comment that will inspire them and help them to feel better about themselves and their lives.

34 Brand Yourself

I realized that the value of the book was not so much in actual sales of the book but in marketing myself.

Brad Dugdale is a Financial Consultant & author of the book 'Let's Save America and Munny Journey.' Visit him at *http://munnyjourney.com.*

As a junior at the University of Montana, I was introduced to the concept of compound interest. On an ordinary day we were asked to calculate what amount of money would need to be saved each month, at our present age, at a return of 12%, to accumulate a million dollars by age 65. I was stunned when I repeatedly performed the calculation and came up with an answer of only $85 a month.

This revelation changed my life and set me on a career as a financial advisor. It also gave me a passion for financial education and a mission to make sure every young person understood the immense benefit that time gave them in creating wealth. It encouraged me to write my first book, *'Let's Save America, 9 lessons to financial success,'* published in 2000.

I, of course, had visions of selling hundreds of thousands of copies because I was sure the country was ready for this message and would share it with others. I wasn't so focused on the amount of money I could make with book sales, but with the way America would change after reading this book. The massive book sales never came. My investment business, however, grew in a spectacular and unexpected way.

I realized that the value of the book was not so much in actual sales of the book but in marketing myself. In addition to trying to get the book in the hands of young people I began to view the book as a business card. I sent copies to clients with teenagers, to business owners in search of financial education tools for their kids (and employees), to service organizations and to teachers. I carried a copy with me wherever I went. I gave out copies when I went to speak to students and social organizations. The speaking engagements increased, the referrals from other clients and professionals picked up and my team doubled our investments under management in about five years. There are now over 10,000 copies of my book in the hands of people across the United States and I am having more printed.

In 2008, I published my second book, 'Munny Journey, a Keepsake Journal for Baby's First Money.' I created this book because I was looking for a new way to explain the concept of compound interest and show how powerful it can be starting from birth. The book is part "keepsake" with pages for baby's first dollar, first savings account and first investment. It is also a financial education tool, showing parents how they can create financial security for a child for as little as a dollar a day.

After being out for only a couple of months, a major Credit Union in the West has ordered 2,500 copies and I have conducted interviews on TV and radio stations across the country. I am firmly established as a financial expert and proponent of financial education in my local market, which leads to more speaking engagements, more referrals and longer term relationships with clients.

My ultimate goal with both books is to change the savings and investing habits of Americans. I want people to be financially independent. I want them to get out of debt and stay out of debt. I want them to enjoy a comfortable retirement. That has always been and will continue to be my driving force. It may also be the reason that these books are proving to be so successful in terms of ultimate value to my business. It has been a nice unintended consequence of trying to improve the lives of others.

35 Expand Your Marketing Platform

My book has become an amazing marketing tool and has helped to propel my career to new and exciting heights. My only regret is that I didn't write it 20 years ago!

Curtis Arnold is Editor-in-Chief and public face of CardRatings.com and author of the book 'How You Can Profit from Credit Cards: Using Credit to Improve Your Financial Life and Bottom Line.' Visit him at http://CardRatings.com.

I had often heard that having a book that you can claim as your own is the ultimate business card, but thought this saying was somewhat of a cliché. While I certainly didn't have any grandiose hopes of getting rich by writing my first book entitled *'How You Can Profit from Credit Cards,'* I did hope that it would open up some professional and media opportunities for me when it was published in June of 2008. To my pleasant surprise, in the course of just a few months, the positive impact of my book on my career has far exceeded my initial expectations. My book has become an amazing marketing tool and has helped to propel my career to new and exciting heights. My only regret is that I didn't write it 20 years ago!

As the founder of CardRatings.com, the most comprehensive source for comparing credit card offers, I have had literally hundreds of opportunities over the years to interact with media outlets and I've been viewed as a leading national expert on credit issues. While I enjoyed a great deal of success prior to writing my book, the book has opened many doors that I would have never been able to walk through otherwise. This is particularly true when it comes to media exposure. For example, soon after publication, I was interviewed on Oprah's XM radio show by Jean Chatzky. Jean is Financial Editor for NBC's Today Show and a contributor to Oprah's television show. At about the same time, I did a live interview on Fox Business at the bar of the renowned Waldorf Astoria hotel (interesting interview, believe me!).

Media interest in the book has also been expressed by such respected publications as the *Wall Street Journal*, *Money Magazine*, *Smart Money* and *Kiplinger's*. All in all, press inquiries have been very robust and have resulted in millions of Americans being exposed to my expertise and to CardRatings.com. And while it's hard to quantify the exact revenue impact of this exposure on our business, it is no doubt quite significant.

Beyond the amazing media and professional exposure that my book has yielded, the most exciting benefits for me are those which are less tangible. The inherent credibility associated with being an author, for example, definitely translates into a strong competitive advantage. Similarly, respect from your peers and other academic types is a good thing. It's hard to put a price tag on these type of benefits—to borrow a phrase from MasterCard, they are indeed priceless.

I have become so convinced of the value of being an author that I've already agreed to co-author my second book titled '*The Complete Idiot's Guide to Person-to-Person Lending*' (Penguin Group USA, April 2009). I'm very excited about this book and the fact that it will be part of the popular *Complete Idiot's Guide* series. And, as you might have guessed, the fact that I was already a published author was certainly instrumental in helping me secure this book deal.

Each new day seems to bring more amazing opportunities. Given what has transpired in the course of just a few months, I can only imagine what the future holds. The life of an author is indeed a splendid thing! What more can I say?

Section V
Marketing

Once you have your book, there are a number applications and approaches that can be taken for the book to help you. Here are a handful of stories.

Rule 36: Create a Bundled Offer

Rule 37: To Give Is to Receive...

Rule 38: Use Books to Educate Your Staff

Rule 39: Educate For a High-Involvement Sale

Rule 40: Farm Your Existing Network

Rule 41: Tie Your Book Into Today's Hot Topics

Create a Bundled Offer

While sales have not been anywhere near the book itself in terms of quantity and units, we have made a nice little profit from the bundle selling 40 in the first four months generating over $12K in revenue.

Brian Lawley is President and Founder of the 280 Group, former President of the Silicon Valley Product Management Association and author of the books 'Expert Product Management' and 'Expert Product Management Toolkit Bundle.' Visit him at http://280group.com.

About two years ago I decided to write a book about the profession of Product Management. Since there are very few resources for learning Product Management, and I already had established channels for reaching the Product Management community, I knew that it would be fairly simple to market and that I would likely sell a reasonable number of copies.

The goal of the book was to capture some of my expertise and use it as a proof point of why my company is the best in the world at what we do. I already had a ten-year track record, dozens of clients (including many well-known companies such as SAP, Nokia, Palm, Adobe, Intel and others) and testimonials, success stories and other marketing ammunition. I knew that writing a book is not a way to make much money. I have seen many authors delude themselves and think they are going to do very well, only to be disappointed. Knowing that, I wanted to make sure that I got a very fair deal from a publisher that would support me so that I would be set up to at least break even.

I chose Happy About as my publisher because I had known Mitchell Levy, the CEO, personally for several years and because their publishing terms were better than the other places I investigated. They had a pre-determined method for bringing books quickly to market. I had the book almost finished, so we were able to fast-track the process and get the book to market within months.

The results were excellent. The book is the best-selling Product Management book on the market, we have gotten significant visibility and we give a copy to CEOs when we are delivering proposals. We received also some inquiries as a result of the book, which resulted in additional business. In the consulting business one large deal with a client can result in tens of thousands of dollars of profit, so this made doing the book worthwhile. That said, the sales of the book alone have already paid for the initial investment and marketing dollars we have spent promoting it.

If this is all that had happened, I would have considered it a success. However, after the book was out for a while I decided to create a second version of it called the *Expert Product Management Toolkit Bundle*.' Over the past ten years, I had spent several thousand hours creating a series of 280 Group Toolkits, which include narrated on-demand training, templates, samples and white papers. I decided to make a modified version of the book and include the templates as a bundle and sell it for a much higher price ($349). The toolkits are $99 each, so the customer would get a great discount ($420 value for $349).

We launched the bundle about two months later and have been pleasantly surprised. While sales have not been anywhere near the book itself in terms of quantity and units, we have made a nice little profit from the bundle selling 40 in the first four months, generating over $12K in revenue. The simple economics of the book industry and the pricing means that for every bundle we sell, we make much more and would have to sell a lot of books to match the profit.

The great thing about all of this is that it easily gave us a second book to use for marketing while at the same time leveraging the hard work we had done in the past to create the toolkits. It was a win-win for both our company and the publisher. It's amazing that we can sell a $349 book on Amazon (34 of the 40 sales)!

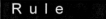
37

To Give Is to Receive...

He encouraged me to send out 5–7 books a day to prospects, journalist, and corporations. Once I started sharing my books, my business grew like gangbusters.

Patrick Snow is a publishing/book coach and author of the book 'Creating Your Own Destiny' which is an international bestseller with over 125,000 copies sold in numerous languages. Visit him at http://createyourowndestiny.com.

I started speaking when I was 18 (22 years ago) and gave three hundred speeches without getting paid. In 1996, I had an epiphany—Why don't I to try to make money speaking?

I graduated in 1991 from the University of Montana and was in corporate sales from 1991 to 2001. I was typically in the top 10%, making the President's Club and maxing out the compensation plan. That said, because of 9/11, I was laid off in 2001, and laid off again in 2002. Finally fed up with the corporate rat race, in 2004 (at age 36) I quit my job to pursue my passion full time.

When looking at the big names that make money speaking, all of them started off self-publishing their own books: Stephen Covey, Tony Robbins, Zig Zigler, Jay Conrad Levinson, and others. In my studies, I learned from self-publishing coach Dan Poynter that writing a best-selling book is like raising a child. It may take nine months to write, then another 18 years to be successful. So I decided to be in it for the long term.

After publishing my book, I had a book release party—which went great—and it's been a great ride since. A lesson I learned is to quickly write and release the book. Having one is so amazing.

Then update and re-release it each year with new content. I started with a 140-page book in paperback form, now it's a 300-page hardcover.

My book has sold over 125,000 copies since I first published it. The first 40,000 was fairly easy once I figured out the trick. At first, I went door to door to different bookstores in Washington. The bookstore owners would say, "'We'll take two on consignment." I would write an invoice with a 40% discount and soon realized that this was not the way to go. Selling books in bookstores was not an approach that would work for me. I needed to sell books in volume. As it worked out, I was able to sell 25,000 to Amway, 10,000 to Nutrition For Life and 15,000 to Stores Online. I didn't make much money per book, but sold large quantities to potential clients.

I went to a National Speakers Association (NSA) conference and ran into a speaker who sold 250,000 copies of his book. His first question was, "How many books are you giving away daily?" I said 1. He encouraged me to send out 5–7 books a day to prospects, journalist, and corporations. Once I started sharing my books, my business grew like gangbusters. Since publishing my book, I've had 900 paid speaking engagements for as much as $14,000 and have coached over 125 clients. My current speaking fee is $20,000.

A business card is nothing more than a 1-penny lead-generating tool. There's nothing on it. There's no content. A book is nothing more than an extension of a business card. For me, it's a relatively inexpensive business card that's a $25 gift. I've given away 2–3K copies to date and will continue to give away as many as possible as it drives business my way.

38 Use Books to Educate Your Staff

Why reinvent the wheel? We believe in books and put our money behind using them to train our employees.

Chad Melvin is currently the manager of corporate training at Aflac, Inc. Visit Aflac at http://aflac.com.

Take care of your employees and they will take care of your customers and your business. At Aflac, we believe it is easier to get better at what you are good at than try to improve something you have a weakness in. We use books to inspire and to teach and to strengthen our employees' skills and our company. A key book used in training employees is *'Now Discover Your Strengths.'* Using this book as a template, our employees take an online survey in which their top five strengths are identified from a battery of 34. They then combine in teams, teams which are blind to the top five strengths of each individual. Teams participate in a Family Feud style of game and then the teams are disbanded and regrouped with different members.

Aflac conducts between 200 and 300 courses for their employees each year, using 14 trainers to develop and facilitate the programs. On average, each employee takes roughly 40 hours of classroom training to enhance his personal and professional growth each year.

For seven years in a row, Aflac has been named one of the top organizations by Training Magazine. Additionally, Aflac has been listed by Fortune Magazine as one of the Top 50 places to work, one of the Top 50 Places for Minorities to work and one of the Top Companies by Working Mothers Magazine.

We continuously look at ways to promote lifelong learning and develop programs to encourage it. Again, books are a big part of that at every level of the organization. The training organization does not take a cookie cutter approach, but customizes or ties training to a specific business objective. For example, when we developed a strategic planning department, we brought members in for the team from many different areas of the company. We had to utilize unique, new methods as they worked together to plan the department's vision and mission.

Aflac's leadership academy focuses on executives, managers and supervisors. '*Good to Great*,' as well as the '*21 Laws of Leadership*' are incorporated into the academy classes. Cross utilization of these classes for leadership development ensures that the bench with the next wave of Aflac leaders is ready. The website for Aflac field agents also suggests books to read for personal and professional growth.

Training the field force takes on a different approach. Besides offering online courses and a list of books, we offer additional courses tailored to our independent agents and collaborate with our strategic leadership to eliminate any gaps which may exist at the divisional level.

Our employees who process or "touch" policies, undergo a four-week training course through Columbus Technical College where they earn the Certified Health and Life Insurance Specialist (CHLIS) designation. This course covers HIPPA Requirements, customer service, medical terminology, and other regulations in the insurance industry. Additional job specific training happens after they join Aflac.

To help our partner in learning, the Aflac Foundation recently gave $1 million to Columbus Technical College, which was earmarked for a new library.

History has proven that this emphasis on learning works. We have a unique culture with adaptable people who are looking for the next greatest thing and who are committed to making that happen.

Why reinvent the wheel? We believe in books and put our money behind using them to train our employees.

39 Educate For a High-Involvement Sale

By all predetermined measures, the endeavor has been a success for myself and for OneAccord... I've turned prospective clients into paying clients.

Paul Travis, an interim marketing executive and partner with OneAccord, co-authored the book 'Leadership on Demand: How Smart CEO's Tap Interim Management to Drive Revenue.' Visit him at http://60-Second-Marketing.com.

The challenge kept coming up in internal discussion: "Our value proposition is powerful but not self-evident—how do we communicate the bigger story?" Reflecting on my branding study with an anthropology professor at the Harvard Business School, I saw the opportunity to use a *book* rather than another brochure or white paper. What does one think of the contents of the bag one leaves a trade show with? *Propaganda*. In contrast, what do we think a library is filled with? *Information*.

So a few of the partners at OneAccord LLC collaborated on a book aimed at Presidents, COO's, CEO's, and outside Directors of emerging and mid-market companies. Our nationwide firm positions itself as a 'Catalyst for Revenue Growth'—providing interim executive talent in the sales and marketing realm. Our goals with the book were to:

- Communicate the OneAccord value proposition and return-on-investment
- Highlight *both* successes and failures (more learning happens with the latter)
- Demonstrate credibility and instill confidence in the reader

- Be readable on a plane ride, i.e. not 392 pages
- Drive interest in our services without being a blatant advertisement
- Serve a bigger universe than just ourselves

While most of these points are straightforward, the latter deserves elaboration. We're championing a new way of engaging seasoned expertise, rather than promoting *ourselves* as 'the answer'. We may learn that other interim management practitioners start promoting Leadership on Demand (L.O.D) as well (if anything, we've been *too subtle* about the book being from 'OneAccord').

Note that revenue is not mentioned as a goal. While we wanted to cover ongoing costs of selling the book, operating the corresponding website, etc., we knew that first-time authors rarely made enough to 'pay' for the hundreds and hundreds of hours that go into the creative process.

By all predetermined measures, the endeavor has been a success—for myself and for OneAccord. In addition to hearing from longtime friends (professionals in their own right) saying 'I finally understand what it is you do,' I've turned prospective clients into paying clients by letting them consume the philosophy themselves.

In the months since L.O.D. was published, partners with OneAccord have held four speaking engagements with professional associations or complementary firms, where the book has been sold in the back of the room or the wholesale price was included in the event cost. This is a win/win/win, being unique for most associations and attendees (and, of course, reinforcing our uniqueness in the marketplace).

Our referral sources who read the book are *far* more knowledgeable about recognizing a potential introduction, where one might have 'slipped away' beforehand. And because many people define 'marketing' very differently, the case studies in L.O.D. help referral sources to see how our practice focus differs from, say, a graphic design firm or a market research firm.

It's working. After mailing the book to the Managing Partner of Accenture in a Midwest market recently, one of our partners in the region received an appreciative reply with a meeting request to talk about a specific situation!

40 Farm Your Existing Network

Even those who already knew me now had marketing material (the book) to share with top management of their company.

Chris Stiehl is the author of Pain Killer Marketing, a teacher at UC-San Diego and consultant on "Voice of the Customer" projects. Visit him at http://stiehlworks.com.

I worked for 30 years helping businesses understand their customers and design products and services for them. I did such work for Wyle Laboratories, Polaroid Corporation, the Cadillac Division of General Motors and Pacific Gas & Electric Company. I decided I would have more fun, and make more money, if I could start doing such work as a consultant. When I began working for myself, several former colleagues and co-workers thought enough of me to give me work, but networking can only take you so far. How do you market yourself to other people and companies who do not know you directly?

The more I studied how gurus and consultants marketed themselves successfully, the more I realized that they had external credibility, usually an award or a published book as well as an affiliation with one or more universities. I had been teaching everywhere I lived, from Harvard University and Northeastern University in the Boston area to the University of California, San Diego. I had been part of a team that had won the Malcolm Baldridge National Quality Award while I worked at Cadillac in 1990. I also realized that I was ready to spend more time teaching other companies how to do what I do and talking about my work. I had been at several major companies at times of competition and change. Thus, I had learned a lot and had a lot to share.

I began seriously considering writing a book based upon lessons that I had learned in industry. I began writing for websites and blogs. I began publishing a newsletter with key ideas related to satisfying customers. After a year or so, I realized that I had created the backbone of the book with all of the articles and essays that I had written.

At one of my frequent business speeches to an association of entrepreneurs, one of the people who approached me with questions and comments was a publisher. I showed him the outline of my book and he agreed to publish it!

I began discussing the upcoming book launch on the Internet and at my presentations. The buzz marketing that was created led to the book achieving "bestseller" status on Barnes & Noble.com before it was published. I began to receive visits to my website and telephone calls from people whom I had never met. This continued as the book launched. The book gave me instant credibility with both new clients and old. Even those who already knew me now had marketing material (the book) to share with top management of their company. This led to paid opportunities to speak to corporate meetings and I gained more projects. It was almost as if I was a preferred vendor because I had published a book.

Suddenly, important business and industry groups began to ask if they could book me as a speaker. I had approached some of these groups in the past with little to show for it. Now they were looking for me! I have more projects and more speaking engagements than I have ever had in 10 years of consulting. What surprised me was getting more opportunities even from people whom I already knew, rather than just from new contacts created by the book.

I would strongly encourage small businesses and potential gurus to publish a book.

41

Tie Your Book Into Today's Hot Topics

Publishing a book isn't news...But, you can use the book to comment upon the news and build your reach and reputation.

Liz Goodgold is a branding expert, motivational speaker, and author of 'DUH! Marketing: 99 Monstrous Missteps You Can Use to Learn, Laugh, and 'Grow Your Business' and 'Red Fire Branding: Creating a Hot Personal Brand so that You have Customers for Life.' Visit her at http://redfirebranding.com.

In 1998, I unveiled my new company, The Nuancing Group, a brand-consulting firm to focus on the nuances of branding. I moved from Chicago to San Diego with a detailed business plan, a trademarked name, and a unique point of difference. In fact, I had everything right except one essential ingredient: clients!

To satisfy that need, I immediately embarked upon a crusade of ruthless self-promotion. I started pitching to reporters the wild components our company considers in creating brand names. Within four days, I had hooked a reporter. My story and photo appeared on the front page of the *San Diego Business Journal*. Within two hours of the publication reaching subscribers, my phone started ringing. And, by week's end, I had signed a massive project with HNC Software, now part of Fair, Isaac, the FICO score company. If one article could bring prosperity, I thought a continuous stream of publicity could command business success. Moreover, if Mr. Blackwell or Joan Rivers could get plenty of press kvetching about wardrobes, we could garner as much interest in the business world by analyzing the worst marketing missteps of the month. Voila! The DUH! Marketing Awards e-newsletter was launched.

In February 2001, the first newsletter went out as a cut and pasted Word document to all 300 members of my database. We hit the jackpot! Brandweek was interested in reprinting the Awards and the broadcast media started calling, including CNN. Although the media called, it wasn't sustainable. I appeared on TV as the "creator of the DUH! Marketing Awards", but I couldn't' seem to be the "go to" person for the media about marketing. I hoped that adding "author" to my credentials would change that perception.

I started compiling the best of the DUH! Awards together in 2005 and the book was finally published in July 2006. I thought this book would change the world. I thought it would change my world. I mailed the book with a press release to over 100 publications with an out-of-pocket cost exceeding $4,000! I received a total of zero responses and zero reviews. I finally learned a key lesson: publishing a book isn't news unless it's about a wizard named Harry Potter. But, you can use the book to comment upon the news and build your reach and reputation.

By October 2006, I was tying my book into every conceivable marketing event in the news. Within one month, I had made over 50 TV and radio appearances. Within one year, it would climb into the hundreds. Most importantly, my reputation was established. TV translated into revenue. Radio translated into speaking assignments and speaking assignments propelled sales of the book. I then turned every speaking gig into an opportunity to record the speech and package and sell it as well. By 2007, I moved from selling one book with an average sale of $29.95 to "marketing toolkits" with an average sale of $199.95! Today, that figure is up to $399.00. My speaking fees doubled and I was able to sign my next book on personal branding with a major publisher within 10 days of submitting a proposal.

As I look back, my only regret is that I didn't publish the book sooner. Sometimes "done is better than perfect" is a perfectly appropriate strategy.

42

These Are My Rules. What Are Yours?

I really enjoyed collecting these stories. People have done some amazing things with books. I don't want to stop. To that end, I'd like to hear your story whether it be as an author or a corporation. I've created two blogs to continue the process of hearing and sharing stories on how books have helped individuals and corporations success. Please visit either of these two blogs and submit your story there or email me at info@happyabout.info.

- http://authorthoughtleadership.com

- http://corporatethoughtleadership.com

I'd also like to encourage you to write a book or have one of our ghostwriting companies write a book for you. The best way to start is to fill out the six questions we ask prospective authors. You can find them at this URL. Please email your responses to the email address above. I'll make sure that one of our staff gives you a call to have a robust conversation about you and your book.

- http://superstarpress.com/six_questions.pdf

I hope you enjoyed this book and were inspired to write one (or a couple more) books yourself. If we can be of assistance in any way, please don't hesitate to contact me. Best of luck in all that you do.

Mitchell Levy

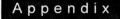

Appendix

A Authors Bios/Photos

This appendix contains those authors that have contributed to this book. They have great stories that truly demonstrate the value of the "printed" word!

Beth Shaw (Rule 5), President and Founder of YogaFit, started the company in 1994. The YogaFit Teacher Training program began in 1997, but after Beth wrote her first book titled '*Beth Shaw's YogaFit*' in 2001, the company took off. The book was a great alternative for people who could not make it to classes or trainings because it is so well written and easy to comprehend. YogaFit became the largest yoga education program in the country. Beth is now an internationally renowned exercise expert who has trained more than 75,000 fitness instructors on six continents. She is the publisher of *Angles* magazine, which is distributed to yoga fitness enthusiasts and instructors. Shaw and YogaFit have been showcased in numerous fitness magazines as well as *Time, More, Entrepreneur, Yoga Journal,* and *USA Today.* She has also been featured on CNBC, CNN, NBC, CBS, E Style Channel, Showtime, and *Donny Deutsch's Big Idea.* You can visit her at http://yogafit.com.

BJ Gallagher (Rule 14) is an inspirational author, speaker, and story-teller. Her books, keynote speeches, and workshops are designed to educate, entertain, and enlighten people—consistently focusing on the "power of positive *doing*." In addition to '*A Peacock in the Land of Penguins*,' she has written fourteen books, including:

- *YES Lives in the Land of NO: A Tale of Triumph Over Negativity*

- *A True Friend...Is Someone Just Like You*

- *What Would Buddha do at Work?*

- *Everything I Need to Know I Learned from Other Women*

Her client list includes: IBM, Chrysler, Chevron, Southern California Edison, the Los Angeles Times, Phoenix Newspapers Inc., American Press Institute, Atlanta Journal-Constitution, Raytheon, John Deere Credit, TRW, Farm Credit Services of America, U.S. Department of Interior, Marathon Realty (Canada), and many others. You may visit her at http://peacockproductions.com or call 323-227-6205 or email PeacockHQ@aol.com.

Bonnie Ross-Parker (Rule 31), a.k.a., America's Connection Diva, is an award wining, multi-dimensional business women/entrepreneur with a background in education, franchise development, publishing, mentorship, network marketing and community development. She combines vision with a unique set of skills. Formerly the Associate Publisher of The Gazette Newspaper/Atlanta, she focuses her energies on supporting women. Awards include the Athena Award—an honor designated to acknowledge women of leadership in cities throughout the United States, The International Toastmaster's annual Communication & Leadership Award and recognition by the Women's Leadership Exchange, a New York based organization, as an Influential Woman of Georgia. Passionate about enriching the lives of business women, in 2002, Bonnie licensed The Joy of Connecting® for professional women, entrepreneurs and business owners to share resources, establish and strengthen relationships and to grow their businesses by networking with one another. Several of her articles on owning one's own business and entrepreneurship have appeared in publications including: *Wealth Building, Home Business Magazine, Business to Business* and *Entrepreneur's Business Start-Ups*. You may visit her at http://BonnieRossParker.com, http://TheJOYofConnecting.com.

Brad Dugdale (Rule 34) is a veteran financial consultant with over 25 years experience. He is the senior partner on a team that manages over $300 million in assets for clients throughout the United States. Brad is a financial literacy expert, speaker and author of two books. His latest book is titled '*Munny Journey, a Keepsake Journal for Baby's First Money.*' It is a keepsake and educational tool showing parents how to start a child on the path to financial security. He believes that people should strive to be financially independent not to be "rich" but to have choice, opportunity and the ability to create a better world through giving. Visit the book at http://munnyjourney.com.

Brian Lawley (Rule 36) is the President and Founder of the 280 Group (http://280group.com), former President of the Silicon Valley Product Management Association and author of the books '*Expert Product Management*' and '*Expert Product Management Toolkit Bundle.*' During his twenty-year career in Product Management he has defined, launched and marketed over fifty successful products. He is the author of the book '*Expert Product Management: Advanced Techniques, Tips & Strategies for Product Management & Product Marketing.*' In 2008 he won the Product Management Excellence Award for Thought Leadership by the Association of International Product Marketing & Management. Mr. Lawley is a Certified Product Manager (CPM) and Certified Product Marketing Manager (CPMM). He earned an MBA with honors from San Jose State University and a Bachelor's Degree in Management Science from the University of California at San Diego.

Chad Melvin (Rule 38) is currently the Manager of Corporate Training at Aflac (http://aflac.com). He has over 14 years' experience in classroom instruction and is certified in Change Management through Prosci. Melvin has served as the Director of Training for Computer Networking Solutions, and worked for seven years as a corporate trainer and courseware developer for US Airways Corporate Training. Melvin holds a Bachelor's degree in Organizational Leadership from Fort Hays State University. He is also in the final stages of completing his Master's in Adult Education at The University of Georgia.

Chris Stiehl (Rule 40) is an author, teacher and consultant. He has won several awards for his work, including being on the team at Cadillac that won the Malcolm Baldridge National Quality Award in 1990. Chris helps companies understand what their customers want through "Voice of the Customer" projects, and he helps them develop metrics and strategies for success. His client list includes Cisco Systems, the LifeScan Division of Johnson & Johnson, Palm, Pfizer, Flowserve, Zeiss, Meditec and many more. His clients have learned how to focus on what is most important to their customers and deliver the products and services that win in the marketplace. You may visit him at http://stiehlworks.com.

Curtis Arnold (Rule 35) is CEO and Founder of CardRatings.com, the most comprehensive source for comparing credit card offers. He is considered a national expert on consumer credit issues and is regularly featured by national media outlets including The Wall Street Journal, The Today Show (NBC), Good Morning America, The Early Show (CBS), USA Today, PBS, Money and SmartMoney Magazines, MSNBC, NPR, The New York Times, Fox Business, Oprah and Friends and The Washington Post. Arnold is also a noted author. In June, 2008, he published '*How You Can Profit from Credit Cards: Using Credit to Improve Your Financial Life and Bottom Line*' by FT Press. He is also co-authoring a book on social lending entitled '*The Complete Idiot's Guide to Person-to-Person Lending*' (Alpha Books/Pengiun Group USA, April 2009), which will be part of the popular *Complete Idiot's Guide to...*series of reference books, and is a contributor to *The Ultimate Allowance* (InnerWealth Publishing, 2008). Finally, Arnold has a particular interest in students and serves as the co-chair of the Arkansas chapter of the Jump$tart Coalition for Financial Literacy, a national non-profit organization that seeks to improve the personal financial literacy of young adults. You may visit him at http://CardRatings.com.

Dianna Booher (Rule 13), MA, CSP, CPAE works with organizations to increase their productivity and effectiveness through better oral, written, interpersonal, and cross-functional communication. As a prolific author of 44 books, she has published with Simon & Schuster/Pocket Books, Warner, Random House, and McGraw-Hill.

Her latest books include '*The Voice of Authority: 10 Communication Strategies Every Leader Needs to Know,*' '*Booher's Rules of Business Grammar: 101 Fast and Easy Way to Correct the Most Common Errors,*' '*Speak with Confidence,*' '*E-Writing: 21st-Century Tools for Effective Communication,*' and '*Communicate with Confidence.*' Good Morning America, CNN, *USA Today, The Wall Street Journal, The New York Times, The Washington Post*, Forbes.com, NPR, CNBC, *Investor's Business Daily*, and Bloomberg have interviewed her for critical opinions on workplace communication. *Executive Excellence Publishing* recently named her as one of the Top 100 Thought Leaders and one of the Top 100 Minds on Personal Development. You may visit her http://booher.com.

Elinor Stutz (Rule 8), CEO of Smooth Sale and author, transformed her highly successful sales career into a sales training company. Past clients included Fortune 100 companies. Smooth Sale, LLC, trains sales teams and entrepreneurs on how to relationship sell to build a thriving business. She also delivers motivational speaking, licensing and products. Elinor's book, '*Nice Girls DO Get The Sale*,' translated into multiple languages, sells worldwide and helped launch the "Sweet Success Book Club." You may visit her at http://smoothsale.net.

Guy Maddalone (Rule27) is the Founder and CEO of GTM Payroll Services/A New England Nanny and author of '*How to Hire a Nanny.*' Guy conducts seminars nationwide on entrepreneurship, household employment, labor, payroll, taxes and human resources; and is a work/life consultant for GE and Textron, among other corporations. Guy founded GTM Payroll Services to provide payroll & tax administration for households; and later expanded services to include business payroll as a complement to the company's core focus. GTM continues to be a leader among national household payroll and tax providers and in 2007 and 2008, GTM was named to INC Magazine's prestigious INC 5000 list. GTM Payroll Services has ranked among Upstate New York's Top 25 Fastest Growing Companies for five consecutive years, and is frequently cited/interviewed/profiled in *The Wall Street Journal*, the *New York Times*, *Parents' Magazine*, NPR and CNN Money. Under Guy's leadership, GTM has been a long-time supporter of The Make A Wish Foundation and other children's charities; which ties into the company's focus of giving back to the community. A graduate of Siena College, Guy serves as a member of the Siena College Associate Board of Trustees. Guy resides in upstate New York with his wife and three children, and is a long-time household employer. You may visit him at http://gtm.com.

Jason Alba (Rule 23) is the CEO and creator of JibberJobber.com, and author of '*I'm on LinkedIn—Now What???*' After a corporate downsizing impacted Jason in 2006, he experienced firsthand the difficulties of conducting a job search. Drawing on his extensive computer software and IT experience, Jason analyzed the job search process and developed JibberJobber.com, the gold standard in career management technology. Jason specializes in social media, with an emphasis on getting professional or business value out of various social tools. Jason maintains four blogs, including http://JibberJobber.com/blog, and is co-author of '*I'm on Facebook—Now What???*'

Jay Conrad Levinson (Rule 2) is the author of the best selling marketing series in history, '*Guerrilla Marketing*,' plus 30 other books. His books have sold 20 million copies worldwide. His guerrilla concepts have influenced marketing so much that today his books appear in 57 languages and are required reading in many MBA programs worldwide. Jay is the Chairman of Guerrilla Marketing International, a marketing partner of Adobe and Apple. He has served on the Microsoft Small Business Council. His Guerrilla Marketing is a series of books, audiotapes, videotapes, a CD-ROM, an Internet website, and an online marketing advancement called The Guerrilla Marketing Association (http://guerrillamarketingassociation.com) —which is an interactive marketing support system for small business.

Dr. Jay P. Granat (Rule 33), Psychotherapist, Hypnotherapist, Author, Lecturer, Coach of Champions, and Founder of StayInTheZone.com is a psychotherapist with 24 years of clinical experience. He has several years of experience with psychology in sports and exercise and has coached thousands of golfers, tennis players, baseball players, basketball players, martial artists, bowlers, fencers, football players, boxers and figure skaters. His clients have included professional athletes, student-athletes, doctors, lawyers, salespeople, traders and some of America's largest corporations. Dr. Granat, has written several mental training in sports books and has lectured extensively on performance enhancement. He is past Vice-President of the New York Society for Ericksonian Psychotherapy and Hypnosis and a university professor. You may visit him at http://StayInTheZone.com.

Jen Blackert (Rule 9) is an author, speaker and strategic success coach. She has personally taught hundreds of individuals her unique principles and approach to massive success. Her principle system called The Simple Way, is based on time-honored universal wisdoms. Jen has authored of several books, and programs, including '*Seven Dragons: A Guide To A Limitless Mind*,' '*Simple Marketing: The Simple Way to Big Business Growth*' and '*Discover Your Inner Strengths*' co-authored with Steven Covey and Ken Blanchard. Her mission is to help busy entrepreneurs and professionals tap into their infinite power and focus on high return on investment strategies so they can take their business to the multiple 7-figures they desire. You may visit her at http://jenblackert.com.

Jim Muehlhausen (Rule 12) CPA, JD is President of CEO Focus (http://ceofocus.com) and author of '*The 51 Fatal Business Errors and How to Avoid Them.*' After graduating from college, Jim became the youngest franchisee in Meineke Discount Muffler history (1987–1991). He sold that business and founded an automotive aftermarket manufacturing concern. During his 9-year tenure, the company achieved recognition from Michael Porter of the Harvard Business School and Inc. Magazine in the IC 100 Fastest Growing Businesses. Over the past eight years, Jim has personally coached hundreds of business owners in over 3500 face-to-face coaching sessions and has clients in North America, Europe, Asia, and the Middle East. He serves on several non-profit and company boards of directors as well as serving as an adjunct professor of business at the University of Indianapolis. He has had articles feature in numerous publications including Businessweek.com, *Entrepreneur, Inc.,* Indianapolis Business Journal, *The Small Business Report, Undercar Digest, Digitrends* and *NAICC Legal Journal.*

JoAnn Mills Laing (Rule 3) is Group President Of First Advantage's Employer Service Group. As President of Information Strategies, Inc., JoAnn put together an information company (http://hsafinder.com) serving more than seven million monthly readers in healthcare, HR, functional and sector areas as well as small and medium size business leaders. The author of two books on HSAs, she is a nationally known authority on HSAs.JoAnn has global work and living experience with four public companies including managing billion plus P&Ls, as well as driving smaller enterprises to liquidity events. She is an active member of international boards. As Chairman of a premier online Audience Development Company, she took the company from idea to profitability and its purchase/IPO. She is a graduate of Syracuse University's Whitman School of Management and holds an MBA from The Harvard Business School.

John Honeycutt (Rule 15) is an accomplished management consultant, entrepreneur and marketing professional. With over 20 total years of know-how, he has counseled Fortune 500 executives across all major industries in both the U.S. and abroad—including 18 years of combined experience with Accenture, Capgemini, Deloitte, and as a partner with CSC Consulting Group. With post-graduate credentials from Cornell University's School of Industrial and Labor Relations and a Master of Science in Management, Computers and Systems, Honeycutt weaves a rich foundation of scholarly insight into his practical on-the-ground approach. When not consulting, he composes and performs music and has contributed his talent to noble causes including Texas Women in Film and the Flight 93 Memorial. He lives in Flower Mound, Texas, with his wife, Jennifer, and teenage children, Danielle and James. You may visit him at http://xbig6.com.

Joshua Estrin (Rule 26) is CEO of Concepts In Success, a consumer marketing and branding firm and author of the book *'Shut Up! And Listen To Yourself.'* Joshua holds a dual MS in Psychotherapy and Human Behavior from Columbia University and has been seen on CNN, FOX, E!, The WB and Good Morning America as well as featured in The NY TIMES, SELF, MORE, LATINA, INC and *Entrepreneur.* As CEO of Concepts In Success, a nationally recognized PR/Marketing firm for Fortune 500 Companies. He is also the author of the acclaimed *Anti Self Help Books, 'Shut Up! and Listen to Yourself!'* He may visit him at http://conceptsinsuccess.com or email jestrin@conceptsinsuccess.com.

Joyce Schwarz (Rule 11) is a futurist, new company launch consultant and Hollywood strategist. Best-selling author of several of the earliest books on new media/multimedia and other books including '*Successful Recareering: When Just Another Job Is Not Enough*' and Tech TV's '*Cutting the Cord: Guide to Going Wireless*.' Visit her at http://joycecom.com, http://hollywood2020.net, http://ihaveavision.org.

Judith E. Glaser (Rule 28) is one of the most innovative and pioneering change agents in the consulting industry. She is the world's leading authority on *WE-centric Leadership*, and refers to herself as an Organizational Anthropologist. Through her dynamic, interactive and provocative keynotes and leadership summits, she has introduced her powerful transformative technologies to CEO's and their teams at major Fortune 500 companies. In 2007 Benchmark launched the *Creating WE Institute* to offer new partnering and research opportunities to enable clients to expand *WE-centric* thinking in their organizations. You may visit her at http://benchmarkcommunicationsinc.com.

Laura Lowell, Executive Editor of the 42 Rules Series (http://42rules.com), is passionate about helping companies be heard; to get the right message to the right customer at the right time. As a sought after consultant, author, and speaker in Silicon Valley, Laura has shared her pragmatic approach to marketing with hundreds of individuals and companies. Prior to launching Impact Marketing Group, Laura held executive positions with Hewlett-Packard, Intel and IBM. Her degree in International Relations prepared her for work assignments in Hong Kong and London. She received her MBA from UC Berkeley, Haas School of Business, with an emphasis on marketing and entrepreneurship. She lives in Los Gatos, California, with her husband Rick, their two daughters, and their dog.

Lisa DiTullio (Rule 24) is a leading force in project and business management. She is the principal of Lisa DiTullio & Associates, a training and consulting practice dedicated to introducing project management as a business competency, enabling organizations to improve decision-making, instill accountability and enhance communications. Lisa is a recognized international speaker in her field—scores of organizations from college campuses to governmental agencies to Fortune 100 companies—have gained from Lisa's insights and tell-it-like-it-is keynotes and workshops. She is the editor of *ProjectBestPractices*, a quarterly newsletter from ProjectWorld, a regular blogger for the Silicon ValleyPM and ProjectConnections sites, and a contributor to *PM Network Magazine*. She's also the author of '*Simple Solutions: How Enterprise Project Management Supported Harvard Pilgrim Health Care's Journey from Near Collapse to #1.*' Lisa is currently writing her next book. You may visit her at http://lisaditullio.com.

Liz Goodgold (Rule 41) is a fiery redhead with a world-renown reputation for delivering whip smart branding strategies to thousands of entrepreneurs and executives each year. She consistently delivers bullet-tested strategies to audiences around the globe based upon her work with Quaker Oats, Univision, Sharp HealthCare, ProFlowers.com, and MusicMatch. An often-quoted expert, Liz has appeared in over 500 media outlets including ABC, CBS, NBC, CNN, PBS, *The New York Times*, and *The Wall Street Journal*. She was also the branding columnist for *Entrepreneur* magazine and is the author of '*DUH! Marketing: 99 Monstrous Missteps You Can Use to Learn, Laugh, and Grow Your Business*' and '*Red Fire Branding: Creating a Hot Personal Brand so that You have Customers for Life.*' You may visit her at http://redfirebranding.com.

Marc Joseph (Rule 22) is President of Dollardays.com (http://dollardays.com) and author of the book '*The Secrets of Retailing.*' With more than 30 years in the retail and wholesale industry, Marc Joseph is one of the founders of DollarDays International, a premiere online wholesaler that helps small businesses compete against larger enterprises by offering more than 25,000 high-quality goods at closeout and wholesale prices. Joseph has helped to build some of America's most well known retail stores including Federated Department Stores, Crown Books, and Bills, a chain of variety stores in Jackson, Mississippi. He also helped ignite the dollar store trend as the General Merchandise Manager in Everything's A Dollar stores based in Milwaukee. Most recently Joseph started a chain of hair salons in Arizona and built it up to 11 stores before selling them to devote himself full time to DollarDays.

Mark Amtower (Rule 20), Founding Partner at Amtower & Company, is an author, consultant, speaker, CEO coach and radio host focusing on one market for the last twenty-five years—***Global One—doing Business with Government***. Known in Washington, DC, for his all-black attire and extreme candor, Amtower is by far the most influential and candid voice in business-to-government marketing, quoted in over 200 publications, doing interviews on business-talk radio around the country, speaking at 15 conferences and seminars each year. You may visit him at http://FederalDirect.com, http://GovernmentMarketingBestPractices.com.

Marsha Petrie Sue (Rule 10), MBA, Certified Speaking Professional, is the Muhammad Ali of conflict-free communications, leadership excellence, and managing change. She dares people to take personal responsibility for their choices, success, and life. She is original, unique, and a one-of-a-kind professional speaker and author. Whether dealing with employee relationships, increasing productivity or pumping up sales, her guiding principles bring energy and fun to any meeting or event. You may visit her at http://MarshaPetrieSue.com, http://DecontaminateToxicPeople.com.

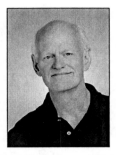

Marshall Goldsmith (Rule 18) is one of the world's foremost authorities in helping leaders achieve positive, measurable change in behavior and has been ranked by the *Wall Street Journal* as one of the "Top 10" consultants in the field of executive development. Marshall's latest book, '*What Got You Here Won't Get You There*,' is a New York Times bestseller, *Wall Street Journal* #1 business book and winner of the Harold Longman Award as the Best Business Book of 2007. He has a Ph.D. from UCLA, teaches executive education at Dartmouths Tuck School and frequently speaks at leading business schools. His work has been recognized by almost every professional organization in his field. In 2006, Alliant International University honored Marshall by naming their schools of business and organizational studies the Marshall Goldsmith School of Management. You may visit him at http://marshallgoldsmith.com.

Michael Soon Lee (Rule 16), MBA, is an expert in marketing and selling to multicultural customers. He is a professional speaker and the author of eight books on diversity. Michael's clients include: Coca-Cola, General Motors, Boeing, Coldwell Banker, Centex Homes, Virginia Tech University, State Farm Insurance, Cedars Sinai Hospital and hundreds of others. You may visit him at http://EthnoConnect.com or call 800-417-7325.

Michelle Dunn (Rule 30) has over 20 years experience in credit and debt collection. She is Founder and President of her Credit & Collections Association, Never Dunn Publishing, LLC, and is a writer, publisher, and consultant. She was recently nominated as one of the Top 5 Women in Collections by Source Media out of NY for 2007 & 2008, won a 2007 Business Excellence Award from the NH Business Review and has been named one of the Top 50 Collection Professionals of 2007. Her second edition of '*Starting a Collection Agency*' won first place in the 2007 New York Book Festival Award in the "How to" category. She has since published a 3rd edition that is a consistent best seller in its category. You may visit her at http://michelledunn.com.

Mike Brooks (Rule 21) is president of Mr. Inside Sales, a Los Angeles based inside sales consulting and training firm that teaches companies and sales reps how to become Top 20% producers. Mike specializes in working with business owners who have under performing outbound or inbound inside sales teams either business-to-business or business-to-consumer. A published author, executive coach and sales trainer, Mike has been teaching the skills, techniques and strategies of Top 20% sales performance for over 25 years. You can visit him at http://MrInsideSales.com.

Patrick Snow (Rule 37) is the best-selling author of *'Creating Your Own Destiny*,' an international speaker, and publishing coach. He has been called the "Dean of Destiny" by high achievers nationwide. His destiny message has been featured numerous national publications including a cover story in *USA Today*. Each year Snow speaks in person to tens of thousands of people and influences the lives of many more through his seminars and coaching programs. Patrick lives with his wife and two sons in Bainbridge Island, WA. You may visit him at http://createyourowndestiny.com.

Paul Travis (Rule 39), an interim marketing executive and partner with OneAccord, co-authored the book *'Leadership on Demand: How Smart CEO's Tap Interim Management to Drive Revenue*.' After his primary roles being father and husband, Paul's quest over 25 years of market- ing, management, technology, and consulting has been driven by this question: *After building customer value and brand loyalty, how can we most effectively scale this business?* He is one of the few people who has launched software products at Microsoft as well as launched natural foods restaurants! Paul is an interim marketing executive and consultant with OneAccord, a national firm based in Seattle. Find the book he co-authored at http://Leadership-On-Demand.com and follow his blog at http://60-Second-Marketing.com.

Paula Jablon and *Ellen Vacco* (Rule 32) have taught English as a Second Language and Adult Basic Education for over twenty years in a variety of academic, workplace and vocational settings. They have conducted workplace needs analyses, developed programs, written material, designed curriculum and trained teachers. They also have presented programs on workplace education to local chambers of commerce, work sites and learning centers as well as to regional, state and national organizations, including a committee of representatives from the Massachusetts and United States Departments of Labor. Their workplace program, conducted in collaboration with the Hudson/Maynard (MA) Chamber of Commerce, received the Adult Education Award in Business/Labor. In addition, they participated in the Massachusetts Frameworks Initiative, the Workplace Education Collaborative (WEC) of the Metro South/West Regional Employment Board (MA), and a workplace study for the Center for Labor Market Studies at Northeastern University. Following the publication of their books, '*At Work in the U.S.*' and '*Conversations for Work*,' Paula and Ellen started a business, ESL Work Solutions (http://eslworksolutions.com). In addition to offering their materials, they conduct workshops for schools, organizations and businesses.

Rajesh Setty (Rule 6) is a serial entrepreneur, investor and author based in Silicon Valley. Rajesh serves as the President and CEO of Suggestica where they build private and public discovery engines using Rawsugar technology. He also serves as the executive chairman of Jiffle where they help solve scheduling problems across companies. Rajesh is involved in several other technology businesses in the US, Europe and India in some combination of investor, founder, advisor and/or an executive. He is a member of the Band of Angels, an angel network in Silicon Valley and Vistage, a worldwide networking organization for CEOs. His last book, *'Beyond Code: Learn to distinguish yourself in 9 simple steps!'* (foreword by Tom Peters), was published in late 2005. You can visit him at http://blog.lifebeyondcode.com.

Robert Van Arlen (Rule 4) is the author of *'Focused Synergy: Orchestrating Your Purpose, Path and Performance,'* His book provides specific guidance on vision and values alignment for individuals and organizations, both of which are critical for unifying and driving successful organizations today. Robert is renowned for his highly engaging speeches and his motivational training and team building programs. He believes that great leaders constantly evolve and that passion is the foundation for contagious success. You can visit him http://robertvanarlen.com.

Sharon Armstrong (Rule 25) is the founder of Sharon Armstrong and Associates and author of three books: '*The Essential HR Handbook*,' published in 2008 by Career Press and co-authored by Barbara Mitchell; '*Stress-free Performance Appraisals*,' co-authored by Madelyn Appelbaum and published by Career Press in 2003; and '*Healing the Canine Within: A Dog's Self-Help Companion*,' published by Ballantine Books in 1998. In 2000, she founded Sharon Armstrong and Associates, a human resources company that works with individuals and organizations to initiate or complete HR projects and conduct training sessions, develop and implement career management plans, and broker HR consultants, coaches, trainers and keynote speakers. You can visit her http://TheEssentialHRHandbook.com.

Shel Horowitz (Rule 19) is a copywriter and award-winning author whose latest books are '*Grassroots Marketing for Authors and Publishers*' (http://grassrootsmarketingforauthors.com) and '*Principled Profit: Marketing That Puts People First*' (http://principledprofit.com). Shel specializes in affordable, ethical, and effective marketing for authors and publishers, small businesses, and nonprofits. He is a popular speaker who has addressed writer and publisher groups around the country. Shel also walks writers through the process of becoming published authors, starting by figuring out which publishing model makes sense and continuing until finished books are in your hand. You can reach him through the contact form at http://frugalmarketing.com or at 413-586-2388.

Steven Wiley (Rule 29) is an entrepreneur, author, and acclaimed international speaker who in 1991 founded The Lincoln Leadership Institute at Gettysburg, an organization that has helped thousands of executives from Fortune 500 companies improve their sales and leadership techniques by using the lessons learned at the Battle of Gettysburg. Wiley also travels around the world delivering a motivational speech that is based on his first book, '*The Human Side of High Performance*.' The second book in a three-part series will arrive in bookstores in 2009. You can visit him at http://lincolnleadershipinstitute.com.

Thomas G. Martin (Rule 17) is the former supervisory federal agent of the U.S. Department of Justice and has over 35 years of professional experience in corporate security and as a private investigator. With his extensive public and private investigation background and a Masters degree in Public Management, Martin is recognized as an expert detective in federal, state, and local courts. He works closely with the legal community throughout Southern California where his services have been respected and relied upon for decades.

Martin has helped locate hundreds of missing persons and runaways for their families and loved ones, and has worked with executives at Fortune 500 and large private companies on matters of fraud, electronic eavesdropping, and security risk analysis. You may visit him at http://martinpi.com.

Vicki Kunkel (Rule 7) is an award-winning social anthropologist who has been recognized as an expert in mass appeal and persuasive communication by several media outlets—including MSNBC, *Entrepreneur*, *Success* and *AP Network News*. She is a former television news anchor, talk show host, current personal branding expert, and freelance social science writer. She has created "sticky" personal brands for national politicians (several Congressional representatives, senators and prominent governors), Fortune 100 CEOs, and lawyers. She has also been called upon to write trial case themes that appeal to our subconscious and activate primal persuasion triggers. You may visit her at http://beapowerplayer.com.

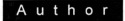

About the Author

Mitchell Levy is CEO and publisher of Happy About (http://happyabout.info), a quick2publish book publisher you should know about if you're an author or are responsible for marketing for your firm. His overarching goal in life has been to put tools in the hands of corporations and individuals to help them be successful.

Author of eight business books, he is also a partner in CXOnetworking and sits on the Board of Directors of Rainmaker Systems (NASDAQ: RMKR). He was the former Chair of four conferences at Comdex; creator of the world-renown E-Commerce Management Program at San Jose State University; and managed the e-commerce component of Sun Microsystem's $3.5 billion supply chain during his nine years there.

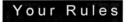
Write Your Own Rules

You can write your own 42 Rules book, and we can help you do it—from initial concept, to writing and editing, to publishing and marketing. If you have a great idea for a 42 Rules book, then we want to hear from you.

As you know, the books in the 42 Rules series are practical guidebooks that focus on a single topic. The books are written in an easy-to-read format that condenses the fundamental elements of the topic into 42 Rules. They use realistic examples to make their point and are fun to read.

Two Kinds of 42 Rules Books

42 Rules books are published in two formats: the single-author book and the contributed-author book. The single-author book is a traditional book written by one author. The contributed-author book (like *42 Rules for Working Moms*) is a compilation of Rules, each written by a different contributor, which support the main topic. If you want to be the sole author of a book or one of its contributors, we can help you succeed!

42 Rules Program

A lot of people would like to write a book, but only a few actually do. Finding a publisher, and distributing and marketing the book are challenges that prevent even the most ambitious of authors to ever get started.

At 42 Rules, we help you focus on and be successful in the writing of your book. Our program concentrates on the following tasks so you don't have to:

- **Publishing:** You receive expert advice and guidance from the Executive Editor, copy editors, technical editors, and cover and layout designers to help you create your book.

- **Distribution:** We distribute your book through the major book distribution channels, like Baker & Taylor and Ingram, Amazon.com, Barnes and Noble, Borders Books, etc.

- **Marketing:** 42 Rules has a full-service marketing program that includes a customized Webpage for you and your book, email registrations and campaigns, blogs, webcasts, media kits and more.

Whether you are writing a single-authored book or a contributed-author book, you will receive editorial support from 42 Rules Executive Editor, Laura Lowell, author of *42 Rules of Marketing*, which was rated Top 5 in Business Humor and Top 25 in Business Marketing on Amazon.com (December 2007), and author and Executive Editor of *42 Rules for Working Moms*.

Accepting Submissions

If you want to be a successful author, we'll provide you the tools to help make it happen. Start today by answering the following questions and visit our website at http://superstarpress.com/ for more information on submitting your 42 Rules book idea.

Super Star Press is now accepting submissions for books in the 42 Rules book series. For more information, email info@superstarpress.com or call 408-257-3000.

Other Happy About Books

Learn the 42 Rules of Marketing!

Compilation of ideas, theories, and practical approaches to marketing challenges that marketers know they should do, but don't always have the time or patience to do.

Paperback $19.95
eBook $11.95

Marketing Thought: Tools, Tactics, and Strategies that Drive Results

This book is all about meeting the needs and wants of the customer.

Paperback $19.95
eBook $11.95

42 Rules of Growing Enterprise Revenue

This book will inspire sales, marketing, and business development executives to re-think old strategies and brainstorm new growth opportunities.

Paperback $19.95
eBook $11.95

Twitter Means Business

For companies unfamiliar with Twitter, this book serves as a field guide. They will get a Twitterverse tour, and learn about the dozens of firms big and small that have harnessed Twitter as a powerful, flexible business tool.

Paperback $19.95
eBook $11.95

Purchase these books at Happy About
http://happyabout.info
or at other online and physical bookstores.

A Message From Super Star Press™

Thank you for your purchase of this 42 Rules Series book. It is available online at:
http://www.happyabout.info/42rules/books-drive-success.php or at other online and physical bookstores. To learn more about contributing to books in the 42 Rules series, check out http://superstarpress.com.

Super Star Press™ is interested in you if you are an author who would like to submit a non-fiction book proposal or a corporation that would like to have a book written for you. Please contact us by email info@superstarpress.com or phone (408-257-3000).

Please contact us for quantity discounts at sales@superstarpress.com

If you want to be informed by email of upcoming books, please email bookupdate@superstarpress.com.

More Praises for 42 Rules for Driving Success with Books

"Having helped connect tens of thousands of experts with the media, I can say one thing for certain, authors have the advantage hands-down. Read this book to see for yourself. If you're a professional service provider or a corporation trying to demonstrate thought leadership, this is a must read!"
Dan Janal, CEO, PR Leads

"'42 Rules for Driving Success With Books' is a must read for any entrepreneur in the advice business. Mitchell Levy has pulled together the ideas from an impressive list of contributors -- heavy hitters who have built their success by writing books. I wish I had read this book prior to writing my first book in 1994. The advice it contains is priceless. This book belongs on the bookshelf -- no, make that on the desk, of any entrepreneur who wants to build his or her personal and professional success."
Bud Bilanich, The Common Sense Guy, author of 'Straight Talk for Success'

"I always say that in order to achieve success you must first build visibility and then credibility; only then can you move forward into profitability. In '42 Rules for Driving Success with Books,' Mitchell Levy explains how becoming a published author is the ultimate way to build visibility and credibility by branding yourself as an expert which will inevitably build your business. Simply put, this book is an essential read for anyone wishing to attain a higher degree of success."
Ivan Misner, NY Times Bestselling author and Founder of BNI

"I've spent my career as a visionary, pioneering in artificial intelligence, ecommerce and most recently personalized medicine. I've always wanted to write a book but somehow never could find the time. I wish I could have read this book 25 years ago. Having your key customers, suppliers, and collaborators drive the core content is a great idea I need to revisit myself, especially since my current focus is collaborative medical research. Seeing the benefits that others have generated from books is motivational. Great job!"
Marty Tenenbaum, Chairman and Chief Scientist, CollabRx

"As the author of 'Championship Networking,' I know exactly how important a book can be as a launching pad to further business success. It worked for me! A book is the ultimate networking and marketing tool, creating a name (i.e., 'branding') for a businessperson or product. As I said in 'Championship Networking,' "You must be noticed by those of influence. Broaden your scope and your visibility . . ." '42 Rules for Driving Success with Books' helps business people recognize the importance of doing just that. Mitchell's '42 Rules' will give you many tools and techniques that will allow you to share your wisdom and expertise with the world."
Eric Shaw, President, New York Credit, Inc. and President, All Cities Network

LaVergne, TN USA
02 October 2009
159751LV00003B/3/P